Sword of the Spirit -
An Offering of Nietzschean Philosophy to the Soldiers of the Third Reich

Compiled by Joachim Schondorff

Translated and Edited by
Dietrich H. Wright

Sword of the Spirit
An Offering of Nietzschean Philosophy
to the Soldiers of the Third Reich

Compiled by Joachim Schondorff

Translated and Edited by
Dietrich H. Wright

ISBN-13: 978-1-913176-61-7

1st German edition published 1940

Sanctuary Press Ltd
71-75 Shelton Street
Covent Garden
London
WC2H 9JQ

www.sanctuarypress.com
Email: info@sanctuarypress.com

Für meine Brünhilde...

To all who contributed to this work, whether by encouragement, thoughtful insight, honest critique or inspiring dialogue, this project would never have come to light without you, thus you will forever have my gratitude. You know who you are. Take my most heartfelt thanks, and enjoy this work.

D. H. W.

Contents

Friedrich Nietzsche in his Prussian Army uniform, 1868.

Bibliography

Found beneath the aphorisms are abbreviations of Nietzsche's works from which the selected texts were taken. The meanings are as follows:

(A) *The Antichrist*

(BT) *The Birth of Tragedy*

(D) *Daybreak*

(EH) *Ecce Homo*

(GE) *Beyond Good and Evil*

(GM) *On the Genealogy of Morals*

(GS) *The Gay Science*

(H) *Human, all too Human*

(N) *Nachlaß, The Innocence of Becoming*

(T) *Twilight of the Idols*

(UM) *The Untimely Meditations*

(WP) *The Will to Power*

(Z) *Thus Spake Zarathustra*

Foreword

When the water hath planks, when gangways and railings o'erspan the stream, verily, he is not believed who then saith: "All is in flux."

But even the simpletons contradict him. "What?" say the simpletons, "all in flux? Planks and railings are still *over* the stream!

"Over the stream all is stable, all the values of things, the bridges and bearings, all 'good' and 'evil': these are all *stable*!"

Cometh, however, the hard winter, the stream-tamer, then learn even the wittiest distrust, and verily, not only the simpletons then say: "Should not everything – *stand still*?"

"Fundamentally standeth everything still" – that is an appropriate winter doctrine, good cheer for an unproductive period, a great comfort for winter-sleepers and fireside-loungers.

"Fundamentally standeth everything still" –: but *contrary* thereto, preacheth the thawing wind!

The thawing wind, a bullock, which is no ploughing bullock – a furious bullock, a destroyer, which with angry horns breaketh the ice! The ice however – *breaketh gangways*!

O my brethren, is not everything *at present in flux*? Have not all railings and gangways fallen into the water? Who would still *hold on* to "good" and "evil?"

Sword of the Spirit

"Woe to us! Hail to us! The thawing wind bloweth!" – Thus preach, my brethren, through all the streets! [(Z)]

Friedrich Nietzsche felt himself to be a "thawing wind" as such. He wanted to be a young, wrathful, clarifying spring storm that could clear away the "winter doctrine" of his time.

Nietzsche lived his life during the time of the civil capitalist civilization at the end of the 19th century and that artificial German culture after 1871, which swayed heavily overjoyed in security, unaware of the near abyss. Amid the shiftiness and frailty of this "modern European" world, a new standard of values and a new hierarchy of men was detected and designed – found here is the epochal meaning of Nietzsche.

He was, of course, not the only one allowed to be the thawing wind to clear away the rotten constructs of inherent prejudices and false ideals – this also arose in our days, in *effect* with Adolf Hitler – though as a "Sword of the Spirit," prepared to destroy any resistance standing in the way of a new path toward the future and wield itself beyond our present days and afar off into the future.

Let this "Sword of the Spirit" accompany the German warriors and soldiers as they help build a new Europe upon the ruins of an old world, and who keenly understand the truth of Nietzsche's words which conclude the following selection:

Brethren, war's the origin
Of happiness on earth!

Joachim Schondorff

Bamberg,
June, 1940

I

History, Culture, Nation

History

You can only explain the past by what is highest in the present. Only by straining the noblest qualities you have to their highest power will you find out what is greatest in the past, most worth knowing and preserving. Like by like! Otherwise you will draw the past to your own level. Do not believe any history that does not spring from the mind of a rare spirit. You will know the quality of the spirit, by its being forced to say something universal, or to repeat something that is known already; the fine historian must have the power of coining the known into a thing never heard before and proclaiming the universal so simply and profoundly that the simple is lost in the profound, and the profound in the simple.[(UM)]

Thus, history is to be written by the man of experience and character. He who has not lived through something greater and nobler than others, will not be able to explain anything great and noble in the past. The language of the past is always oracular: you will only understand it as builders of the future who know the present.[(UM)]

Cheerfulness, a good conscience, belief in the future, the joyful deed, all depend in the individual as well as the nation, on there being a line that divides the visible and clear from the vague and shadowy: we must know the right time to forget as well as the right time to remember; and instinctively see when it is necessary to feel historically, and when unhistorically. This is the point that the reader is asked to consider; that the unhistorical and the historical are equally necessary to the health of an individual, a community, and a system of culture.[(UM)]

The unhistorical is like the surrounding atmosphere that can alone create life, and in whose annihilation life itself disappears. It is true that man can only become man by first suppressing his unhistorical element in his thoughts, comparisons, distinctions, and conclusions, letting a clear sudden light break through these misty clouds by his power of turning the past to the uses of the present. But an excess of history makes him flag again, while without the veil of the unhistorical he would never have the courage to begin. What deeds could man ever have done if he had not been enveloped in the dust-cloud of the unhistorical?[(UM)]

We do need history, but quite differently from the jaded idlers in the garden of knowledge, however grandly they may look down on our rude and unpicturesque requirements. In other words, we need it for life and action, not as a convenient way to avoid life and action, or to excuse a selfish life and a cowardly or base action. We would serve history only so far as it serves life...[(UM)]

History is necessary to the living man in three ways: in relation to his action and struggle, his conservatism and reverence, his suffering and his desire for deliverance. These three relations answer to the three kinds of history – so far as they can be distinguished – the *monumental*, the *antiquarian*, and the *critical.*[(UM)]

Each of the three kinds of history will only flourish in one ground and climate: otherwise it grows to a noxious weed. If the man who will produce something great, have need of the past, he makes himself its master by means of monumental history: the man who can rest content with the traditional and venerable, uses the past as an "antiquarian historian": and only he whose heart is oppressed by an instant need, and who will cast the burden off at any price, feels the want of "critical history," the history that judges and condemns. There is much harm wrought by wrong and thoughtless planting: the critic without the need, the antiquary without piety, the knower of the great deed who cannot be the doer of it, are plants that have grown to weeds, they are torn from their native soil and therefore degenerate.[(UM)]

History is necessary above all to the man of action and power who fights a great fight and needs examples, teachers and comforters; he cannot find them among his contemporaries. It was necessary in this sense to Schiller; for our time is so evil, Goethe says, that the poet meets no nature that will profit him, among living men. Polybius is thinking of the active man when he calls political history the true preparation for governing a state; it is the great teacher, that shows us how to bear steadfastly the reverses of fortune, by reminding us of what others have suffered. Whoever has learned to recognize this meaning in history must hate to see curious tourists and laborious beetle-hunters climbing up the great pyramids of antiquity. He does not wish to meet the idler who is rushing through the picture-galleries of the past for a new distraction or sensation, where he himself is looking for example and encouragement. To avoid being troubled by the weak and hopeless idlers, and those whose apparent activity is merely neurotic, he looks behind him and stays his course towards the goal in order to breathe. His goal is happiness, not perhaps his own, but often the nation's, or humanity's at large: he avoids quietism, and uses history as a weapon against it. For the most part he has no hope of reward except fame, which means the expectation of a niche in the temple of history, where he in his turn may be the consoler and counsellor of posterity. For his orders are that what has once been able to extend the conception of "man" and give it a fairer content, must ever exist for the same office. The great moments in the individual battle form a chain, a high road for humanity through the ages, and the highest points of those vanished moments are yet great and living for men; and this is the fundamental idea of the belief in humanity, that finds a voice in the demand for a "monumental" history.

But the fiercest battle is fought round the demand for greatness to be eternal. Every other living thing cries no. "Away with the monuments," is the watch word. Dull custom fills all the chambers of the world with its meanness, and rises in the thick vapor round anything that is great, barring its way to immortality, blinding and stifling it. And the way passes through mortal brains! Through the brains of sick and short-lived beasts that ever rise to the surface to breathe, and painfully keep off annihilation for a little space. For they wish but one thing: to live at any cost. Who would ever dream of any "monumental history" among them, the hard torch-race that alone gives life to greatness? And yet there are always men awakening, who are strengthened and made happy by gazing on past greatness, as though man's life were a lordly thing, and the fairest fruit of this bitter tree were the knowledge that there was once a man who walked sternly and proudly through this world, another who had pity and loving-kindness, another who lived in contemplation, – but all leaving one truth behind them, that his life is the fairest who thinks least about life. The common man snatches greedily at this little span, with tragic earnestness, but they, on their way to monumental history and immortality, knew how to greet it with Olympic laughter, or at least with a lofty scorn; and they went down to their graves in irony – for what had they to bury? Only what they had always treated as dross, refuse, and vanity, and which now falls into its true home of oblivion, after being so long the sport of their contempt. One thing will live, the sign-manual of their inmost being, the rare flash of light, the deed, the creation; because posterity cannot do without it. In this spiritualized form fame is something more than the sweetest morsel for our egoism, in Schopenhauer's phrase: it is the belief in the oneness and continuity of the great in every age, and a protest against the change and decay of generations.[(UM)]

What is the use to the modern man of this "monumental" contemplation of the past, this preoccupation with the rare and classic? It is the knowledge that the great thing existed and was therefore possible, and so may be possible again. He is heartened on his way; for his doubt in weaker moments, whether his desire be not for the impossible, is struck aside.[(UM)]

Secondly, history is necessary to the man of conservative and reverent nature, who looks back to the origins of his existence with love and trust; through it, he gives thanks for life. He is careful to preserve what survives from ancient days, and will reproduce the conditions of his own upbringing for those who come after him; thus he does life a service. The possession of his ancestors' furniture changes its meaning in his soul: for his soul is rather possessed by it. All that is small and limited, moldy and obsolete, gains a worth and inviolability of its own from the conservative and reverent soul of the antiquary migrating into it, and building a secret nest there. The history of his town becomes the history of himself; he looks on the walls, the turreted gate, the town council, the fair, as an illustrated diary of his youth, and sees himself in it all – his strength, industry, desire, reason, faults and follies. "Here one could live," he says, "as one can live here now – and will go on living; for we are tough folk, and will not be uprooted in the night." And so, with his "we," he surveys the marvelous individual life of the past and identifies himself with the spirit of the house, the family and the city. He greets the soul of his people from afar as his own, across the dim and troubled centuries: his gifts and his virtues lie in such power of feeling and divination, his scent of a half-vanished trail, his instinctive correctness in reading the scribbled past, and understanding at once its palimpsests[1] – nay, its polypsests.[2] Goethe stood with such thoughts before the monument of Erwin von Steinbach: the storm of his feeling rent the historical cloud-veil that hung between them, and he saw the German work for the first time "coming from the stern, rough, German soul." This was the road that the Italians of the Renaissance travelled, the spirit that reawakened the ancient Italic genius in their poets to "a wondrous echo of the immemorial lyre," as Jacob Burckhardt says. But the greatest value of this antiquarian spirit of reverence lies in the simple emotions of pleasure and content that it lends to the drab, rough, even painful circumstances of a nation's or individual's life: Niebuhr[3] confesses that he could live happily

1 Palimpsest (from Greek, Palin = again, psen = to wipe away, erase), once described parchment whose print contains an older beneath it.

2 Corresponding Polypsest (Greek Polys = much), repeatedly described parchment.

3 Niebuhr, Barthold Georg, Historian, * 1776 Copenhagen, † 1831 Bonn, founder of historiography, chief work "Roman History," 3 volumes, 1811-32 (here appeared historical source criticism for the first time.)

on a moor among free peasants with a history, and would never feel the want of art. How could history serve life better than by anchoring the less gifted races and peoples to the homes and customs of their ancestors, and keeping them from ranging far afield in search of better, to find only struggle and competition? The influence that ties men down to the same companions and circumstances, to the daily round of toil, to their bare mountain-side, – seems to be selfish and unreasonable: but it is a healthy unreason and of profit to the community; as everyone knows who has clearly realized the terrible consequences of mere desire for migration and adventure, – perhaps in whole peoples, – or who watches the destiny of a nation that has lost confidence in its earlier days, and is given up to a restless cosmopolitanism and an unceasing desire for novelty. The feeling of the tree that clings to its roots, the happiness of knowing one's growth to be not merely arbitrary and fortuitous, but the inheritance, the fruit and blossom of a past, that does not merely justify but crown the present – this is what we nowadays prefer to call the real historical sense.[(UM)]

There is always the danger here, that everything ancient will be regarded as equally venerable, and everything without this respect for antiquity, like a new spirit, rejected as an enemy. The Greeks themselves admitted the archaic style of plastic art by the side of the freer and greater style; and later, did not merely tolerate the pointed nose and the cold mouth, but made them even a canon of taste. If the judgment of a people hardens in this way, and history's service to the past life is to undermine a further and higher life; if the historical sense no longer preserves life, but mummifies it: then the tree dies, unnaturally, from the top downwards, and at last the roots themselves wither. Antiquarian history degenerates from the moment that it no longer gives a soul and inspiration to the fresh life of the present. The spring of piety is dried up, but the learned habit persists without it and revolves complaisantly round its own centre. The horrid spectacle is seen of the mad collector raking over all the dust-heaps of the past. He breathes a moldy air; the antiquarian habit may degrade a considerable talent, a real spiritual need in him, to a mere insatiable curiosity for everything old: he often sinks so low as to be satisfied with any food, and greedily devour all the scraps that fall from the bibliographical Quisquilien.[4]

Even if this degeneration does not take place, and the foundation be not withered on which antiquarian history can alone take root with profit to life: yet there are dangers enough, if it becomes too powerful and invades the territories of the other methods. It only understands how to preserve life, not to create it; and thus always undervalues the present growth, having, unlike monumental history, no certain instinct for it. Thus it hinders the mighty impulse to a new deed and paralyses the doer, who must always as doer, be grazing some piety or other. The fact that it has grown old carries with it a demand for its own immortality. For when one considers the life-history of such an ancient fact, the amount of reverence paid to it for generations – whether it be a custom, a religious creed, or a political principle, – it seems presumptuous, even impious, to replace it by a new fact, and the ancient congregation of pieties by a new piety.*(UM)*

Here we see clearly how necessary a third way of looking at the past is to man, beside the other two. This is the "critical" way; which is also in the service of life. Man must have the strength to break up the past; and apply it too, in order to live. He must bring the past to the bar of judgment, interrogate it remorselessly, and finally condemn it. Every past is worth condemning: this is the rule in mortal affairs, which always contain a large measure of human power and human weakness. It is not justice that sits in judgment here; nor mercy that proclaims the verdict; but only life, the dim, driving force that insatiably desires – itself. Its sentence is always unmerciful, always unjust, as it never flows from a pure fountain of knowledge: though it would generally turn out the same, if Justice herself delivered it. "For everything that is born is *worthy* of being destroyed: better were it then that nothing should be born." It requires great strength to be able to live and forget

4 Quisquilien (Latin) = vanities, odds and ends.

how far life and injustice are one. Luther himself once said that the world only arose by an oversight of God; if he had ever dreamed of heavy ordnance, he would never have created it. The same life that needs forgetfulness, needs sometimes its destruction; for should the injustice of something ever become obvious – a monopoly, a caste, a dynasty for example – the thing deserves to fall. Its past is critically examined, the knife put to its roots, and all the "pieties" are grimly trodden under foot. The process is always dangerous, even for life; and the men or the times that serve life in this way, by judging and annihilating the past, are always dangerous to themselves and others. For as we are merely the resultant of previous generations we are also the resultant of their errors, passions, and crimes: it is impossible to shake off this chain. Though we condemn the errors and think we have escaped them, we cannot escape the fact that we spring from them.[(UM)]

This is how history can serve life. Every man and nation needs a certain knowledge of the past, whether it be through monumental, antiquarian, or critical history, according to his objects, powers, and necessities. The need is not that of the mere thinkers who only look on at life, or the few who desire knowledge and can only be satisfied with knowledge; but it has always a reference to the end of life, and is under its absolute rule and direction. This is the natural relation of an age, a culture and a people to history; hunger is its source, necessity its norm, the inner plastic power assigns its limits. The knowledge of the past is only desired for the service of the future and present, not to weaken the present or undermine a living future. All this is simple as truth itself, and quite convincing to anyone who is not in the toils of "historical deduction."[(UM)]

The fact that the Germans, for a whole century, have devoted themselves more particularly to the study of history, only tends to prove that they are the stemming, retarding and becalming force in the activity of modern society – a circumstance which some, of course, will place to their credit. On the whole, however, it is a dangerous symptom when the mind of a nation turns with preference to the study of the past. It is a sign of flagging strength, of decline and degeneration; it denotes that its people are perilously near to falling victims to the first fever that may happen to be rife – the political fever among others.(UM)

I am always amazed that people never experience hesitance when they gaze afar off into the past. Though historical fever and great momentary vanity exist side by side.(N)

How vastly historical wisdom kills, as Goethe once said: "Then, if I had so clearly known how much excellence spanning centuries and millennia is here, I would not have written a single word, and have done something else." (Unknown)

The unrestrained historical sense, pushed to its logical extreme, uproots the future, because it destroys illusions and robs existing things of the only atmosphere in which they can live. Historical justice, even if practiced conscientiously, with a pure heart, is therefore a dreadful virtue, because it always undermines and ruins the living thing; its judgment always means annihilation. If there be no constructive impulse behind the historical one, if the clearance of rubbish be not merely to leave the ground free for the hopeful living future to build its house, if justice alone be supreme, the creative instinct is sapped and discouraged.(UM)

CULTURE

Culture is, before all things, the unity of artistic style, in every expression of the life of the people. Abundant knowledge and learning, however, are not essential to it, nor are they a sign of its existence; and, at a pinch, they might coexist much more harmoniously with the very opposite of culture – with barbarity: that is to say, with a complete lack of style, or with a riotous jumble of all styles. *(UM)*

In certain epochs the Greeks were in a similar danger of being overwhelmed by what was past and foreign, and perishing on the rock of "history." They never lived proud and untouched. Their "culture" was for a long time a chaos of foreign forms and ideas, – Semitic, Babylonian, Lydian, and Egyptian, – and their religion a battle of all the gods of the East; just as German culture and religion is at present a death-struggle of all foreign nations and bygone times. And yet, Hellenic culture was no mere mechanical unity, thanks to that Delphic oracle.[5] The Greeks gradually learned to organize the chaos, by taking Apollo's advice and thinking back to themselves, to their own true necessities, and letting all the sham necessities go. Thus they again came into possession of themselves, and did not remain long the Epigoni of the whole East, burdened with their inheritance. After that hard fight, they increased and enriched the treasure they had inherited by their obedience to the oracle, and they became the ancestors and models for all the cultured nations of the future.

This is a parable for each one of us: he must organize the chaos in himself by "thinking himself back" to his true needs. He will want all his honesty, all the sturdiness and sincerity in his character to help him to revolt against second-hand thought,

---

5 ...thanks to that Delphic oracle (Delphi, sanctuary of the well-known Delphic oracle, is therefore the most venerated city of Apollo) last but not least, thanks to that Apollonian oracle. For Nietzsche, "the word *'Apollonian'* expresses: the constraint to be absolutely isolated, to the typical 'individual,' to everything that simplifies, distinguishes, and makes strong, salient, definite, and typical: to freedom within the law."*(WP)*

second-hand learning, second-hand action. And he will begin then to understand that culture can be something more than a "decoration of life" – a concealment and disfiguring of it, in other words; for all adornment hides what is adorned. And thus the Greek idea, as against the Roman, will be discovered to him, the idea of culture as a new and finer nature, without distinction of inner and outer, without convention or disguise, as a unity of thought and will, life and appearance. He will learn too, from his own experience, that it was by a greater force of moral character that the Greeks were victorious, and that everything which makes for sincerity is a further step towards true culture, however this sincerity may harm the ideals of education that are reverenced at the time, or even have power to shatter a whole system of merely decorative culture.*(UM)*

The history of the development of culture since the time of the Greeks is short enough, when we take into consideration the actual ground it covers, and ignore the periods during which man stood still, went backwards, hesitated or strayed. The Hellenizing of the world – and to make this possible, the Orientalizing of Hellenism – that double mission of Alexander the Great, still remains the most important event: the old question whether a foreign civilization may be transplanted is still the problem that the peoples of modern times are vainly endeavoring to solve. The rhythmic play of those two factors against each other is the force that has determined the course of history heretofore. Thus Christianity appears, for instance, as a product of Oriental antiquity, which was thought out and pursued to its ultimate conclusions by men, with almost intemperate thoroughness. As its influence began to decay, the power of Hellenic culture was revived, and we are now experiencing phenomena so strange that they would hang in the air as unsolved problems, if it were not possible, by spanning an enormous gulf of time, to show their relation to analogous phenomena in Hellenistic culture. Thus, between Kant and the Eleatics,[6] Schopenhauer

6 Eleatics, Greek philosophy school in Elea (southern Italy) in year 6 B.C., which taught the unity, simplicity and permanence of being.

and Empedocles,[7] Æschylus and Wagner, there is so much relationship, so many things in common, that one is vividly impressed with the very relative nature of all notions of time. It would even seem as if a whole diversity of things were really all of a piece, and that time is only a cloud which makes it hard for our eyes to perceive the oneness of them. In the history of the exact sciences we are perhaps most impressed by the close bond uniting us with the days of Alexander and ancient Greece. The pendulum of history seems merely to have swung back to that point from which it started when it plunged forth into unknown and mysterious distance. The picture represented by our own times is by no means a new one: to the student of history it must always seem as though he were merely in the presence of an old familiar face, the features of which he recognizes. In our time the spirit of Greek culture is scattered broadcast. While forces of all kinds are pressing one upon the other, and the fruits of modern art and science are offering themselves as a means of exchange, the pale outline of Hellenism is beginning to dawn faintly in the distance. The earth which, up to the present, has been more than adequately Orientalized, begins to yearn once more for Hellenism. He who wishes to help her in this respect will certainly need to be gifted for speedy action and to have wings on his heels, in order to synthesize the multitudinous and still undiscovered facts of science and the many conflicting divisions of talent so as to reconnoitre and rule the whole enormous field. It is now necessary that a generation of *anti-Alexanders* should arise, endowed with the supreme strength necessary for gathering up, binding together, and joining the individual threads of the fabric, so as to prevent their being scattered to the four winds. The object is not to cut the Gordian knot of Greek culture after the manner adopted by Alexander, and then to leave its frayed ends fluttering in all directions; it is rather *to bind it after it has been loosed*. That is our task today.[(UM)]

7 Empedocles, Greek philosopher, circa 490 – 430 B.C., taught that there is neither becoming nor decaying in actual significance, but only composition and decomposition, connection and separation from the four inalterable, fixed and eternal elements of fire, air, water and earth.

The enfeebled Greeks have become romanticized, coarsened and decorative, then later accepted as an ally via the decorative culture of enfeebled Christendom, spread with violence by uncivilized peoples – that is the history of western culture.[(N)]

It is a magnificent spectacle: from local interests, from people who are bound to the smallest of fatherlands, from works of art that are taken to a festival for a day, from clear points, thus, a lasting practice of bridging culture between nations and peoples is gradually developed in space and time; the local receives universal, while the momentary receives monumental significance. These corridors in history must be traced; from time to time we hold our breath, as the yarn is spun, and the knots that bind the furthest past to the present are torn so closely! [(N)]

Casting of culture. Culture is molded like a bell within a casing of coarse, ordinary material: falsehood, violence, boundless expansion of every individual ego, every individual nation, have fit this mold. Is now the time to remove it? Has the molten solidified? Have the good, advantageous instincts, along with the habits of more noble minds, become so secure and common, that there is no longer dependence on metaphysics and the errors of religions, nor are severity and violence any longer the strongest bond between man and man, nation and nation? To answer this question, there are no helpful signs from any god: our own insight must decide. Man's rule of the earth must be in the hands of man himself, his 'omniscience' must keep a watchful eye over the further destiny of culture. [(H)]

Let us acknowledge unprejudicedly how every higher civilization hitherto has *originated!* Men with a still natural nature, barbarians in every terrible sense of the word, men of prey, still in possession of unbroken strength of will and desire for power, threw themselves upon weaker, more moral, more peaceful races (perhaps trading or cattle-rearing communities), or upon old mellow civilizations in which the final vital force was flickering out in brilliant fireworks of wit and depravity. At the commencement, the noble caste was always the barbarian caste: their superiority did not consist first of all in their physical, but in their psychical power – they were more *complete* men (which at every point also implies the same as "more complete beasts"). (GE)

The "humanization" of such barbarians, in part due to an unintentional process, which set in motion the approximate determination towards a balance of power, is essentially a debilitating process that occurs at the expense of the instincts which allowed them to triumph and rule in the first place; and while they seized these "humanitarian" virtues, perhaps even with a grand impetuosity in accordance with their "spiritual greed," to overcome old civilizations, arts, religions, they carried out a gradual, backwards process favoring the side of the conquered and enslaved. Within these dimensions, in which the meeker, more humane were stuck, and the more physically strong consequently thrived, thereby evolving the strengthened man, the man-animal with wild desires, the *barbarian*: the barbarian, who one day feels strong enough to resist his humanized, effeminized, rulers. The game begins anew: the origins of a *higher civilization* return once again. (N)

He who rests his hope on a future great man, receives his first "initiation into culture." The sign of this is shame or vexation at one's self, a hatred of one's own narrowness, a sympathy with the genius that ever raises its head again from our misty wastes, a feeling for all that is struggling into life, the conviction that Nature must be helped in her hour of need to press forward to the man, however ill she seem to prosper, whatever success may attend her marvelous forms and projects: so that the men with whom we live are like the debris of some precious sculptures, which cry out – "Come and help us! Put us together, for we long to be complete."(UM)

Without myth each culture loses the healthy, natural power of its creativity: only a horizon defined by myths unifies a whole cultural movement.(BT)

Culture is merely a thin veil above fiery, violent chaos.*(N)*

The cyclops of culture. To behold those deep, furrowed coombs where glaciers have nestled, makes it seem impossible that a time will come when a forested valley with creeks will flourish across the same place. It is no different with the history of mankind: the most barbaric forces beat the path, are highly destructive, but their work was nevertheless necessary, so that later a gentler civilization may build its home. The ghastly energies, those called evil, are the cyclopean architects and road builders of humanity.*(H)*

The Statue of Humanity. The genius of culture does just as Cellini[8] did when he forged his statue of Perseus: the liquid mass appeared alarmingly insufficient, yet he was *determined* to do it: and so he cast into it keys, plates and whatever else fell into his hands. And so does that genius throw in errors, vices, hopes, delusions and other materials of baser as well as nobler metals, as the statue of humanity must emerge completed; what does it matter if inferior material is used here and there? *(H)*

Happiness and Culture. The sight of our childhood neighborhood moves us: the garden house, the church with the graveyard, the pond and the forest – we always look back upon it with suffering. Self-pity seizes us, for all we have suffered through since then! And here everything still stands motionless and eternal: only we are so different, so affected; we even rediscover a few people on whom time has ground its teeth as *little* as it has on an oak tree: farmers, fishermen, forest dwellers – they are the same. To be moved, to feel self-pity in the face of a lower culture is the sign of a higher culture; wherefrom it ensues, that happiness is under no circumstance augmented. He who desires to harvest happiness and contentment from life needs only to stray from the path toward a higher culture.*(H)*

8 Cellini, Benvenuto, Italian. Goldsmith and sculptor, * 1500 † 1571. His bronze statue of Perseus with the head of Medusa stands in the Loggia dei Lanzi in Florence.

A high civilization is a pyramid: it can only stand upon a broad basis, it has for a first pre-requisite a strongly and soundly consolidated mediocrity.[(A)]

The problem of a culture is rarely summarized correctly. It aims not for a people's greatest possible *bliss*, nor is it the unhindered development of *all* their abilities: instead it shows itself in proper *proportions* within those developments. Its goal shows itself excessively in earthly happiness: the production of great works is its goal.[(N)]

Talent is only the requirement for culture. The essence is the development of the archetype. [(N)]

Whereupon should the concept of "cultural advancement" be measured? Every man says *he* stands highest, and *his* ideal is the ideal of mankind.[(N)]

You should not flee towards metaphysics but should instead sacrifice yourselves to the *rising culture*! Thus am I strongly against dreamy idealism.[(N)]

It is the task of a culture to see that greatness in a people appears neither as a hermit nor an exile.[(N)]

To be "*simple and natural*" is the highest and final goal of culture! Meanwhile we want to strive; strive to bind and shape ourselves, so that we may return to simplicity and beauty in the end.[(N)]

Nation & Race

He who hath grown wise concerning old origins, lo, he will at last seek after the fountains of the future and new origins.

O my brethren, not long will it be until *new peoples* shall arise and new fountains shall rush down into new depths.

For the earthquake – it choketh up many wells, it causeth much languishing: but it bringeth also to light inner powers and secrets.

The earthquake discloseth new fountains. In the earthquake of old peoples new fountains burst forth. [(Z)]

Many lands saw Zarathustra, and many peoples: thus he discovered the good and bad of many peoples. No greater power did Zarathustra find on earth than good and bad.

No people could live without first valuing; if a people will maintain itself, however, it must not value as its neighbor valueth.

Much that passed for good with one people was regarded with scorn and contempt by another: thus I found it. Much found I here called bad, which was there decked with purple honors.

Never did the one neighbor understand the other: ever did his soul marvel at his neighbor's delusion and wickedness.

A table of excellencies hangeth over every people. Lo! it is the table of their triumphs; lo! it is the voice of their Will to Power.

It is laudable, what they think hard; what is indispensable and hard they call good; and what relieveth in the direst distress, the unique and hardest of all, – they extol as holy.

Whatever maketh them rule and conquer and shine, to the dismay and envy of their neighbors, they regard as the high and foremost thing, the test and the meaning of all else.

Verily, my brother, if thou knewest but a people's need, its land, its sky, and its neighbor, then wouldst thou divine the law of its surmountings, and why it climbeth up that ladder to its hope.[(Z)]

It is decisive for the fortune of a people and of humanity, that civilization begins at the *right place* – *not* at "soul" (as was the baneful superstition of priests and semi-priests); the right place is body, demeanor, regimen, physiology; the *rest* follows therefrom. It is on that account that the Greeks are the *leading event* in the history of *civilization*: they knew, they *did* what was necessary; Christianity, which despised the body, has hitherto been the greatest misfortune for the human race. [(T)]

Nearly every age and stage of culture has at one time sought with deep displeasure to free itself from the Greeks because in their presence, everything culture achieved for itself, though apparently completely original and wholeheartedly admired, seemed suddenly to lose life, color and wither into a failed caricature. Therefore, time after time sincere anger erupts against this pretentious bunch of people who, for all time, were bold enough to call everything not native "barbaric." Who are they, we ask, who, despite the fact that they only possess an ephemeral[9] historical brilliance, laughably limited institutions, a shaky proficiency in their customs, are even marked with ugly vices, can lay claim to the dignity and exceptionality among peoples who lay genius among the masses? Unfortunately, we were not so lucky to find the cup of hemlock with which we could simply do away with such an entity; for all the poison created by envy, defamation, and anger was not enough to destroy that self-sufficient glory. And so shame and fear is felt before the Greeks, unless truth over all things holds value and dares to acknowledge even this truth; that the Greeks, as charioteers, hold the reins of our own and every culture in their hands, though chariots and horses are almost always too inadequate and inept for the glory

9 Ephemeral (Greek, ephemeral) = temporary, transitory.

of their leaders, who make a sport of driving such a team into an abyss, which they themselves clear with the leap of Achilles. *(BT)*

On the acquired character of the Greeks. We are easily misled by the celebrated clarity, transparency, simplicity and order of the Greeks, also by the crystalline nature and likewise crystalline aesthetic of their works, into believing that it was all simply handed to them: for example, they were unable to write terribly, as Lichtenberg[10] once said. But nothing could be more hasty or untenable. ... Simplicity, flexibility, sobriety were inherent in them and were then *taken* away. The danger of regression into the Asiatic forever loomed over the Greeks, and from time to time they were suddenly engulfed by an overflowing stream of mysticism and wild elemental darkness. We see them sink, we see Europe likewise washed away and drowned, for Europe was very small at that time, but they always surface, like the excellent swimmers and divers they are, the nation of Odysseus. *(H)*

Greek wisdom. With the desire for victory and distinction being an unconquerable force of nature, older and more primal than any attention paid to joy in equality, the Greek state sanctioned athletic and artistic competition among equals, and at that, in a Colosseum where that force could be unleashed without endangering political order. With the final decline of the athletic and artistic contests, the Greek state fell into inner desolation and turmoil. *(H)*

True Heathenism. Perhaps nothing astonishes the observer of the Greek world more than when he learns that the Greeks often held festivals for all their passions, their naturally sinister inclinations and even established an official program in celebration of what was all too human in them: this demonstrates the true heathenism of their world, never comprehended by and never comprehensible to Christianity, which has forever despised and fought it with utmost severity. They determined this all too human essence

10 Lichtenberg, Georg Christoph, * 1742 † 1799, philosopher of the German Enlightenment, a master of brilliantly sharp aphorisms. Cf. Aphorisms, Letters, Writings in the collection (KTA Volume 154).

of theirs to be innate and, instead of cursing it, held it to be a kind of right in second rank through integration within societal and religious customs: yes, indeed, all in man possessing *power* they called godlike and carved it on the walls of their paradise. They did not deny the natural drive that expresses itself in bad qualities, but controlled it, and as soon as they found sufficient protective measures to provide these wild waters with the least harmful means of outflow, they confined it to fixed rituals and days. This is the root of antiquity's moral free mindedness. The evil and suspicious, the animal and backward, even the barbarian, the pre-Greek and Asiatic, all remained in the foundations of Hellenic nature, were all granted a moderate discharge, and their annihilation was not pursued. The entire system of such orders was embraced by the state, which was established to not accommodate certain individuals or castes, but mankind's ordinary qualities. With this structure the Greeks demonstrated that wonderful sense for the typical and factual that later suited them to become natural scientists, historians, geographers and philosophers. It was not a narrow-minded priest or caste dominated moral code that determined the state constitution and state religion: but rather the most comprehensive regard for *all human reality.* Wherefrom did the Greeks attain this freedom, this sense for the real? Perhaps from Homer and the poets before him; for it is indeed the poets, whose natures are not the very wise or just, who possess joy in the real and active *of every sense* and have no want to outright deny evil: they are satisfied if it keeps itself contained and avoids wholesale slaughter or inner contamination – meaning, they think alike with the pioneers of the Greek world, and were their instructors and pathfinders. [(H)]

To scent out "beautiful souls," "golden mediocrities," and other perfections in the Greeks, perhaps to admire in them the repose in grandeur, the ideal disposition, lofty simplicity – from this "lofty simplicity" (a *niaiserie allemande* in the end), I was preserved by the psychologist implanted in my nature. I saw their strongest instinct, the will to power, I saw them quake in presence of the intractable force of this impulse, – I saw all their institutions evolve out of protective measures to secure themselves mutually from their innate *explosive material.* The enormous internal tension then discharged itself externally, in dreadful and reckless hostility: the city communities lacerated themselves in conflict with one another, in order that the citizens of each might find peace within themselves. People required to be strong; danger was close at hand, – it lurked everywhere. The magnificently supple physique, the daring realism and immoralism which belonged to the Hellene, were an *exigency*, not a "temperament." These qualities only came in course of time, they were not there from the beginning. And the Greeks desired naught else but to feel themselves *dominant*, to *show* themselves dominant with their festivals and arts: these things were expedients for self-glorification, under certain circumstances for inspiring terror... *(T)*

The Greek culture rests on the relationship of control of one, slightly numerous, class against four to nine times that many dependents. The masses of Greece were once largely barbarians. How we see the ancients' humanity! *(Unknown)*

A culture of men. Greek culture of the classical era is a culture of men. Concerning women, Pericles[11] says it all with the words of his Funeral Oration: they are at their best when men speak of them as little as possible. The erotic relationship between men and boys was, to a degree which escapes our understanding, the necessary requirement of all male upbringing (similar to how it was with all of us, and for a long time, when higher education was introduced to women only through love affairs and marriage); all powerful idealism of Greek nature threw itself upon this relationship, and young people have likely never since been treated with so much attention and kindness with regard to enhancing the very best in them (*virtus*) as they were in the sixth and fifth centuries – in accordance with Hölderlin's beautiful maxim "love is given best by mortals." The higher the regard paid to this relationship, the less regard was given

11 Pericles, the Athenian statesman, in 431 B.C. wrote a eulogy for the first fallen soldiers of the Peloponnesian war, in which he referred to the widows. Cf. Thucydides, *History of the Peloponnesian War* (KTA Volume 150).

to communication with woman: angled toward child bearing and lust – nothing more was considered; there was no spiritual connection, not even an actual love affair. Considering further that they were excluded from competitions and plays of every kind, only religious cults remained as the sole form of higher discourse for women. If the tragedy of Elektra and Antigone were nonetheless performed on stage, this was *endured* in art, though not wanted in life: just as today we could not bear all the pathos in *life* that we are happy to experience in art. The women had no duty other than to bear handsome, mighty bodies in which the father's character lived on as whole as possible and thereby counteract the nervous strain that was gaining the upper hand in such a highly developed culture. This kept Greek culture young for a relatively long time; for in Greek mothers returned the Greek genius time and again to nature.[*(H)*]

Among the Greeks, from Homer to Pericles, women were always repressed: this belongs to the culture of the Greeks – a certain violence was practiced against mild and soft feelings.[*(N)*]

If we were to correctly interpret the overall life of the Greeks, we would only find its own reflection in the mirror, in which its greatest genius is illumined with bright colors. With the first experience of philosophy on Greek soil, along with the sanction of the seven sages,[12] is a clear and unforgettable stripe on the symbol of the Hellenes. Other peoples have their saints, the Greeks have their sages.[*(N)*]

There can be no doubt that the Greeks sought to interpret, by means of their Dionysian experiences, the final mysteries of the "destiny of the soul" and everything they knew concerning the education and the purification of man, and above all concerning the absolute hierarchy and inequality of value between man and man. There is the deepest experience of all Greeks, which they conceal beneath great silence – *we do not know the Greeks* so

12 The seven sages (of Greece), were statesmen and law-givers in 7 and 6 B.C., whose wisdom of life was passed throughout Hellas via oral tradition.

long as this hidden and subterranean access to them remains obstructed. The indiscreet eyes of scholars will never perceive anything in these things, however much learned energy may have may still have to be expended in the service of this excavation; even the noble zeal of such friends of antiquity as Goethe and Winckelmann, seems to savour somewhat of bad form and of arrogance, precisely in this respect.*(WP)*

The Greeks did not see the Homeric gods standing above them as masters, nor themselves kneeling beneath them as servants, like the Jews did. As it were, they saw only the mirror image of the most successful examples of their own caste, thus an ideal, not an antithesis of their own being. They felt related to them, where there existed a mutual interest, a type of symmetry. Man feels himself noble when he offers himself to such gods and enters into a relationship with them akin to a relationship between lower and higher nobilities... *(H)*

Greek morals were not based on religion, but on the Polis.[13] Every priest had a god, and every god its priest. There were no spokesmen of the entire religion: therefore, no *rank*, likewise no holy document.*(N)*

The human nature of the Hellenes lies in a conscious naïveté, in which, to them, man bares himself via the state, art, partnerships, war, international law, sexual intercourse, discipline, and political parties; it is indeed human nature that bares itself above all and amid all people, but to them, when facing bare inhumanity, that cannot go without indoctrination.*(N)*

How simple the Greeks were in their own conception of themselves! How far we surpass them in knowledge of human nature! However, how labyrinthine our souls and our conceptions seem to us compared to theirs!*(D)*

13 Polis (Greek = City), the City-State was the smallest, but the sole leader of "political" unity in ancient Greece. The full particulars are found in J. Burckhardt's "Greek Cultural History" I (KTA Volume 58)

The Hellene is neither an optimist nor a pessimist. He is essentially *man*, who truly sees the terrible, and unmasked at that. *(N)*

The artists of *life*; they have their gods, so they may live, not so they become estranged to life. *(N)*

Alas, Greek history moves so swiftly! Never since has life been so luxuriously and exorbitantly lived. *(H)*

To assert the Teutons were predetermined and conditioned for Christianity, there can be no greater impudence in such an assertion. If it is so, the antithesis is not only true, but also obvious. Wherefrom should the fabrication of Jesus and Saul, the two very Jewish Jews, who may or may not have existed, be more intimate with the Teutons than with other peoples? *(N)*

A *nihilistic* religion like Christianity, old and rugged enough to have survived every strong instinct and accordingly sprung out of the people, transmitted itself step by step through other spheres of influence, finally within the youth, and even converted people *yet to exist – very odd!* An evening blessing including a shepherd and a grand conclusion preached to barbarians and Teutons! How all must be barbarized and Germanized! And in such a way, *as those* who dreamt of *Valhalla* know, that all the happiness on earth was found in war! A *supra*national religion preached outside of and within chaos, where *yet no* nation has *once* been.*(N)*

It hardly seems possible to transplant a foreign myth with continual success without irreparably damaging the tree via the transplant. Perhaps, in one case, it may be strong and healthy enough to eliminate this foreign element through a violent fight, however, it must consume itself sick and withered, or in diseased overgrowth. We think so highly of the pure and powerful core of German character that we dare to expect of it, above all others, the elimination of forcibly implanted foreign elements, and deem it possible that the German spirit will reclaim itself. Some may perhaps suppose that this spirit must begin its fight by eliminating the Romantic: whereby they may recognize external preparation and encouragement in the triumphant fortitude and bloody glory of the last war. The German must seek the inner necessity in the drive to be worthy of the grand masters on this path, like Luther and our many great artists and poets. But never let him believe he could fight similar fights without the gods of his house, without his mythical homeland, without a "resurrection" of all things German! And if the German should hesitantly look around for a leader who might return him to his long-lost home, whose ways and paths he no longer knows, let him simply listen to the delightfully beckoning call of the Dionysian bird[14] that hovers above him and desires to show him the way.[(BT)]

None shall believe the German spirit has forever lost its mythical homeland when it can still clearly understand the bird calls which sing of that homeland. One day it will find itself awake in the morning light after a deep sleep: then it will slay dragons, defeat treacherous dwarfs and awaken Brunhild – even Wotan's spear will not be able to stop it![(BT)]

I heard, once again for the first time, Richard Wagner's overture to the *Mastersingers*: it is a piece of magnificent, gorgeous, heavy, latter-day art, which has the pride to presuppose two centuries of music as still living, in order that it may be understood: – it is an honor to Germans that such a pride did not miscalculate! What flavors and forces, what seasons and climes do we not find mingled in it! It impresses us at one time as ancient, at another time as foreign, bitter, and too modern, it is as arbitrary as it is pompously traditional, it is not infrequently roguish, still oftener rough and coarse – it has fire and courage, and at the same time the loose, dun-colored skin of fruits which ripen too late. It flows

14 Dionysian Bird, symbolic of the spirit of the Greek god Dionysus. For Nietzsche, Dionysian is "a primal drive to unity, a soaring above personality, the mundane, society, reality, and above the abyss of the ephemeral; the passionately painful sensation of superabundance, in darker, fuller, and more in flux conditions; an ecstatic yea saying to the collective character of life."[(WP)]

broad and full: and suddenly there is a moment of inexplicable hesitation, like a gap that opens between cause and effect, an oppression that makes us dream, almost a nightmare; but already it broadens and widens anew, the old stream of delight – the most manifold delight, – of old and new happiness; including *especially* the joy of the artist in himself, which he refuses to conceal, his astonished, happy cognizance of his mastery and the expedients here employed, the new, newly acquired, imperfectly tested expedients of art which he apparently betrays to us. All in all, however, no beauty, no South, nothing of the delicate southern clearness of the sky, nothing of grace, no dance, hardly a will to logic; a certain clumsiness even, which is also emphasized, as though the artist wished to say to us: "It is part of my intention"; a cumbersome drapery, something arbitrarily barbaric and ceremonious, a flirring of learned and venerable conceits and witticisms; something German in the best and worst sense of the word, something in the German style, manifold, formless, and inexhaustible; a certain German potency and super-plenitude of soul, which is not afraid to hide itself under the *raffinements* of decadence – which, perhaps, feels itself most at ease there; a real, genuine token of the German soul, which is at the same time young and aged, too ripe and yet still too rich in futurity. This kind of music expresses best what I think of the Germans: they belong to the day before yesterday and the day after tomorrow – *they have as yet no today.*[(GE)]

The German soul is above all manifold, varied in its source, aggregated and superimposed, rather than actually built: this is owing to its origin. A German who would embolden himself to assert: "Two souls, alas, dwell in my breast," would make a bad guess at the truth, or, more correctly, he would come far short of the truth about the number of souls.[(GE)]

The German soul has passages and galleries in it, there are caves, hiding-places, and dungeons therein; its disorder has much of the charm of the mysterious; the German is well acquainted with the by-paths to chaos. And as everything loves its symbol, so the German loves the clouds and all that is obscure, evolving, crepuscular, damp, and shrouded: it seems to him that everything uncertain, undeveloped, self-displacing, and growing is "deep." The German himself does not *exist*: he is *becoming*, he is "developing himself."[(GE)]

Is it true that *bad style* belongs to German nature? Or is it a sign that it is incomplete? It is indeed so: that which is *German* has yet to completely emerge. In hindsight there is nothing to learn: one must trust in his own power. *German nature has yet to arrive, it must first become; it must first be born so that it is, above all, certain and sincere before itself. However, every birth is painful and violent.* [(N)]

The Germans *are* not yet anything, but they are *becoming* something; that is why they have not yet any culture; that is why they cannot yet have any culture! They are not yet anything: that means they are all kinds of things. They are *becoming* something: that means they will one day cease from being all kinds of things. The latter is at bottom only a wish, scarcely a hope yet. Fortunately it is a wish with which one can live, a question of will, of work, of discipline, a question of training, as also of resentment, of longing, of privation, of discomfort – yea, even of bitterness – in short, we Germans *will* get something out of ourselves, something that has not yet been wanted of us – we want something *more*!

That this "German, as he is not as yet" – has a right to something better than the present German "culture"; that all who wish to become something better, must wax angry when they perceive a sort of contentment, an impudent "setting-oneself-at-ease," or "a process of self-censing," in this quarter: that is my second principle, in regard to which my opinions have not yet changed.[(WP)]

Until now there was no German culture. There is no objection to the fact that there were great hermits in Germany (Goethe for example): for they had their own culture. Surrounding them presently, like mighty, stubborn, isolated crags, lay the residual German nature as *their antithesis*, like a soft, boggy, unstable ground upon which every step and turn the world left lingering "forms" and "impressions" – German education was a thing without character, a near indefinite resilience. [(N)]

When, from beneath the first layer of turmoil after the emergence of the last great war, a French scholar called the Germans barbarians and accused them of lacking culture, the Germans listened keenly enough to regard this as thoroughly evil, and many journalists gave them the opportunity to brightly polish the rusty armor of their culture and flaunt their assurance of victory with it. The German exhausts himself with assurance that the Germans are the most teachable, educated, gentle and virtuous people in the world: all alone against accusations of cannibalism and piracy, he feels adequately safe. Then when a voice called out from beyond the canal and the honorable Carlyle openly expressed appreciation for every German quality, consecrating victory on their behalf, it was purely about German culture, and following its success it was sure to be innocent to speak about the victory of German culture. Now, when some Germans have the time, they hurl that word at us in order that we must once more acknowledge the fact that there surely are a few who know the Frenchman was right: the Germans are barbarians, despite every humane quality. If one must wish them, the barbarians, victory, it is not simply because they are barbarians, but rather because the hope of an emerging culture sanctifies the Germans, though no consideration is given to a degenerate and utterly spent culture: not the woman who allows the child to degenerate, but rather the one who will give birth, is holy to the law. The fact that they are otherwise still barbarians was Goethe's opinion, who grew old enough to be permitted to speak these truths of the Germans, and on whose words I allow my meditations to connect, with no desire or allowance given to any others. One evening, he said to Eckermann, "we have indeed capably cultivated for a century, but still a few more centuries must pass ere so much spirit and higher culture penetrates and becomes universal among our countrymen, so that one will be able to say of them, it is long since they were barbarians." (N)

The profound, icy mistrust which the German provokes, as soon as he arrives at power, – even at the present time, – is always still an aftermath of that inextinguishable horror with which for whole centuries Europe has regarded the wrath of the blonde Teuton beast.(GM)

The only productive *political* power in Germany, that we need not designate to anyone, has achieved victory in the most incredible way, and henceforth it will master German essence down to the atom. This fact is highly significant, because in that power something will decay – that decay we hate. It is the true enemy of every deep philosophy and artful expression, a diseased state, which primarily German essence has suffered since the French revolution, and still suffers in recurring hauntings of arthritic tremors, along with the best mannered German natures. It is completely hidden from the masses so that everyone suffers – it carries its name with the disdainful desecration of a word spoken with good intentions, "liberalism." With the fabricated idea "dignity of all people," under the "common name of all people," liberalism will build itself, and along with its crassier brother it will turn its gaze to the point where once implied power had sprouted... (N)

"Man must have something he can *unconditionally* obey" – this is a German sensation, a piece of German consistency: it is the basis of all German moral teaching. How different an impression we feel, when we stand before antique morality! Those Greek thinkers, however different they may appear as individuals, seem, as moralists, like a gymnastics teacher speaking to his pupil: "Come forth! Follow me! Submit to my discipline! You may then succeed and carry a prize before all the Hellenes." Personal distinction is antique virtue. To submit and follow, openly or in secret, is German virtue.

But now, what if the German for once, as sometimes happens, stumbles into a state in which he is capable of *great things*? When the *exceptional* hour, the hour of disobedience, strikes? Schopenhauer was wrong when he said the only advantage Germans had over other nations was that more atheists were among them than anywhere else, but I know, when the German stumbles into the aforementioned state, he *lifts himself above morality*! How should he not? He must now do something new, namely command – be it himself or others! But it was not his German morality that taught him to command! German morality forgot it! [(D)]

The small baseness of the German soul was not and is not the consequence of the system of small states: for it is well known that the inhabitants of much smaller states were proud and independent: and it is not a large state that frees souls making them more manly. In whose soul the servile command, "thou shalt and must kneel!" is obeyed, in whose body there is an involuntary bowing to honorary titles, orders, and glances from above – such a man in an "Empire" will only bow more deeply and lick the boot more passionately in the presence of the greater sovereign than in the presence of the lesser: of this there are no doubts. Still, we see that aristocratic self-sufficiency in the lower classes of Italians; manly discipline and self-confidence remain a part of the long history of their country: they are virtues that once *manifested themselves before* their very eyes. A poor Venetian gondolier makes a far better figure than a true privy councilor from Berlin, and is a better man in the end. This is obvious to anyone. Just ask the women.[(N)]

Can we be interested in this German Empire? Where are the new *ideas*? Is it a mere consolidation of power? We are worse off if it does not know what it wants. *Peace* and subversion are no politics I have any respect for. Sovereignty and bringing the highest ideals to triumph – that is the sole interest I have in Germany.[(N)]

German Culture as it once was. When Germans began to be interesting to other European nations, as it happened not long ago, it was because of a culture they no longer possess, which they blindly shook off as though it were an illness. … In the meantime, it cannot be denied that German culture fooled Europeans by competitively sparking interest out of imitation and appropriation that was unworthy of interest anyway. Today let us look at Schiller, Wilhelm von Humboldt, Schleiermacher, Hegel, and Schelling, read their correspondence and familiarize ourselves with their large circle of followers: what do they have in common? What is it about them that seems to us, as we are today, so insufferable, so touching and pitiful? Firstly, their yearning to appear morally *excited* at all costs; then, their desire for glittering, boneless generalities, beside their intentions to see everything (characters, passions, ages, morals) in as beautiful a light as possible – "beautiful," unfortunately in the sense of a murky and bad taste that nevertheless boasts of Greek ancestry. It is a soft, benign, glistening idealism which wants, above all, to wield noble gestures and a noble voice, a desire as presumptuous as it is harmless, infused with sincere hatred for "cold" or "dry" reality, for anatomy, for wholehearted passion, for every kind of philosophical abstinence and skepticism, but especially for natural science, except when it is subject to be utilized as religious symbolism. Goethe observed these events in his own way, by standing aside, mildly reluctant and remaining silent, ever determined to follow his own, better path. Later on, Schopenhauer also noticed them, and to him much of the real world, along with its devilry, had become visible again. What he had to say of it was as crude as it was enthusiastic: for this devilry had its *beauty*! And what was it that so misled foreigners that they did not see German culture the way Goethe and Schopenhauer did, or did they simply disregard it? It was the dull sheen, the mysterious shimmer of the milky way, that lit up this culture: when they saw it, foreigners said: "that is far from us. Our senses of sight, hearing, understanding, joy, and evaluation cannot reach that far; but those may be stars! Could the Germans have quietly discovered a corner of the heavens and settled there? We must work to get closer to the Germans." And closer they got: but hardly had they done so when these same Germans began exerting themselves to dull the shimmer of the milky way, for they knew too well that they were not in the heavens, but in a cloud! (D)

I am only speaking, directly, about the Germans of the present day, who have had to suffer more than other people from the feebleness of personality and the opposition of substance and form. "Form" generally implies for us some convention, disguise or hypocrisy, and if not hated, is at any rate not loved. We have an extraordinary fear of both the word convention and the thing. This fear drove the German from the French school; for he wished to become more natural, and therefore more German. But he seems to have come to a false conclusion with his "therefore." First he ran away from his school of convention, and went by any road he liked: he has come ultimately to imitate voluntarily in a slovenly fashion, what he imitated painfully and often successfully before. So now the lazy fellow lives under French conventions that are actually incorrect: his manner of walking shows it, his conversation and dress, his general way of life. In the belief that he was returning to Nature, he merely followed caprice and comfort, with the smallest possible amount of self-control. Go through any German town; you will see conventions that are nothing but the negative aspect of the national characteristics of foreign states. Everything is colorless, worn out, shoddy and ill-copied. Everyone acts at his own sweet will – which is not strong or serious will – on laws dictated by the universal rush and the general desire for comfort. A dress that made no head ache in its inventing and wasted no time in the making, borrowed from foreign models and imperfectly copied, is regarded as an important contribution to German fashion. The sense of form is ironically disclaimed by the people for they have the "sense of substance": they are famous for their cult of "inwardness."

But there is also a famous danger in their "inwardness": the internal substance cannot be seen from the outside, and so may one day take the opportunity of vanishing, and no one notices its absence, any more than its presence before. One may think the German people to be very far from this danger: yet the foreigner will have some warrant for his reproach that our inward life is too weak and ill-organized to provide a form and external expression for itself. It may in rare cases show itself finely receptive, earnest and powerful, richer perhaps than the inward life of other peoples: but, taken as a whole, it remains weak, as all its fine threads are not tied together in one strong knot. The visible action is not the self-manifestation of the inward life, but only a weak and crude attempt of a single thread to make a show of representing the whole.*(UM)*

German Hopes. – Do not let us forget that the names of peoples are generally names of reproach. The Tartars, for example, according to their name, are the "the dogs"; they were so christened by the Chinese. "*Deutschen*" (Germans) means originally "heathen": it is thus that the Goths after their conversion named the great mass of their unbaptized fellow-tribes, according to the indication in their translation of the Septuagint,[15] in which the heathen are designated by the word which in Greek signifies "the nations." (See Ulfilas.[16]) It might still be possible for the Germans to make an honorable name ultimately out of their old name of reproach, by becoming the first *non-Christian* nation of Europe; for which purpose Schopenhauer, to their honor, regarded them as highly qualified. The work of *Luther* would thus be consummated, – he who taught them to be anti-Roman, and to say: "Here *I* stand! *I* cannot do otherwise!"*(GS)*

I do not understand how a German could ever feel *Christian*... *(A)*

They are an unassuming and fundamentally mediocre species of men, these utilitarian[17] Englishmen, and, as already remarked, in so far as they are tedious, one cannot think highly enough of

15 Septuaginta (Latin, "Seventy"), term for the alleged 72 Greek men who produced the first translation of the Old Testament.

16 Ulfilas, * 310 † 383, Gothic Bishop who translated the Bible into Gothic.

17 Utilitarian (Latin) = attention to usage.

their utility.[18] One ought even to *encourage* them, as has been partially attempted in the following rhymes:

Hail, ye worthies, barrow-wheeling,
"Longer – better," aye revealing,
Stiffer aye in the head and knee;
Unenraptured, never jesting,
Mediocre everlasting
Sans génie et sans esprit![19] *(GE)*

England's small-minded spirit is now the greatest danger on earth. I see more of an inclination towards greatness in the sentiment of Russian Nihilists than those of English Utilitarians. *(N)*

Not a soul believes England is strong enough to play out her old role for so much as another 50 years.*(N)*

"People are equal," "the good of the community comes before the good of the few," "through the good of the few the common good will be necessarily and most suitably boosted" and "the better off the few are, the greater the welfare of the masses" – this is the general ignorance stemming from England. This is herd-instinct put into words to grasp.*(N)*

In England for every little emancipation from divinity, people have to re-acquire respectability by becoming moral fanatics in an awe-inspiring manner.*(T)*

The Englishman, more gloomy, sensual, headstrong, and brutal than the German – is for that very reason, as the baser of the two, also the most pious: he has all the *more need* of Christianity. To finer nostrils, this English Christianity itself has still a characteristic English taint of spleen and alcoholic excess, for which, owing to good reasons, it is used as an antidote – the

18 Utility = usefulness, profitableness.

19 Sans génie et sans esprit (French) = without mind and spirit.

finer poison to neutralize the coarser: a finer form of poisoning is in fact a step towards spiritualization. The English coarseness and rustic demureness is still most satisfactorily disguised by Christian pantomime, and by praying and psalm-singing (or, more correctly, it is thereby explained and differently expressed) ; and for the herd of drunkards and rakes who formerly learned moral grunting under the influence of Methodism (and more recently as the "Salvation Army"), a penitential fit may really be the relatively highest manifestation of "humanity" to which they can be elevated: so much may reasonably be admitted. That, however, which offends even in the humanest Englishman is his lack of music, to speak figuratively (and also literally): he has neither rhythm nor dance in the movements of his soul and body; indeed, not even the desire for rhythm and dance, for "music." Listen to him speaking; look at the most beautiful Englishwoman *walking* – in no country on earth are there more beautiful doves and swans; finally, listen to them singing! But I ask too much...[(GE)]

Finally, let it not be forgotten that the English, with their profound mediocrity, brought about once before a general depression of European intelligence. What is called "modern ideas," or "the ideas of the eighteenth century," or "French ideas" – that, consequently, against which the *German* mind rose up with profound disgust – is of English origin, there is no doubt about it. The French were only the apes and actors of these ideas, their best soldiers, and likewise, alas! their first and profoundest *victims;* for owing to the diabolical Anglomania of "modern ideas," the *âme française*[20] has in the end become so thin and emaciated, that at present one recalls its sixteenth and seventeenth centuries, its profound, passionate strength, its inventive excellency, almost with disbelief. One must, however, maintain this verdict of historical justice in a determined manner, and defend it against present prejudices and appearances: the European *noblesse* – of sentiment, taste, and manners, taking the word in every high sense – is the work and invention of *France;*

20 âme française (French) = the French soul.

the European ignobleness, the plebeianism of modern ideas – is *England's* work and invention.(GE)

The Desire for Perfect Opponents. The French have undeniably been the *most Christian* nation on earth: not because the faith of the masses was stronger in France than elsewhere, but because there, the most difficult Christian ideals were transformed into men, not remaining mere ideas, approaches, or half-measures. There stands Pascal,[21] with the first of all Christians in unity of embers, spirit and integrity, and consider what all had to be united! There stands Fénelon,[22] with the perfect and charming expression of *ecclesiastical culture* in all its strength: a happy medium which an historian may be inclined to determine as something impossible, whereas it was only something unspeakably difficult and improbable. There stands Madame de Guyon[23] with her peers, the French Quietists: and all the eloquence and heat of the apostle Paul yearned to discover in the sublime, loving, silent and enraptured semi-godlike state of the Christian has here become truth and, at the same time delayed that Jewish intrusiveness which Paul stripped of his God thanks to a genuine, feminine, fine and noble old French naïveté in word and gesture. There stands the founder of the Trappist monasteries,[24] he, who took the ascetic ideal of Christianity with dire seriousness and did so, not as an exception among Frenchmen, but rightly as a Frenchman: for his dark creation remained powerful and at home only among Frenchmen; it followed them from Alsace to Algeria. Let us not forget the Huguenots: the union of warlike and industrious

21 Pascal, Blaise, * 1623 † 1662. French mathematician and philosopher, whose thoughts culminated in a completely self-awarded prize from god.

22 Fénelon, Francois, * 1651 † 1715, French writer, later an archbishop, worked effectively with his moral-pedagogical writings, especially with the much read coming of age story "The Adventures of Telemachus", strongly refined, though churchly influenced educational background.

23 Guyon, Madame Jeanne Marie, * 1648 † 1717, French mystic and quietist, which means a representative of the doctrine, that valued the passive giving in the will of god more than that of the Catholic church's mandated religious practices, penned many writings.

24 Founders of the Trappist monasteries: Jean Le Bouthillier de Rancé, * 1626 † 1700, Abbot of the cloister Soligny-La-Trappe, who, in 1665 founded the monastic order of the "Trappists," which observed vows of silence, vegetarian living, sleep in full clothing, and were never buried in coffins.

sensibilities, of more refined morals and Christian severity, was never more beautifully represented before the Huguenots. And in Port-Royal[25] the great world of Christian scholarship bloomed for the final time: and blossoms are understood by great men in France more so than elsewhere. Far from being superficial, a great Frenchman nevertheless seeks to maintain his surface, that being a natural skin to house his content and depths – while the depths of a great German are usually kept enclosed in a peculiar capsule, as an elixir which seeks to protect itself from light and careless hands by the hard strangeness of its shell. And now, guess why the nation possessing these perfect types of Christians was determined to also breed perfect antitheses of unchristian free spirits! The French free spirit fought within itself against great men, not merely with dogmas and sublime monstrosities, as did the free spirits of other nations.*(D)*

The disease of the will is diffused unequally over Europe; it is worst and most varied where civilization has longest prevailed; it decreases according as "the barbarian" still – or again – asserts his claims under the loose drapery of Western culture. It is therefore in the France of today, as can be readily disclosed and comprehended, that the will is most infirm.*(GE)*

The power to will and to persist is … strongest and most surprising of all in that immense middle empire where Europe as it were flows back to Asia – namely, in Russia. There the power to will has been long stored up and accumulated, there the will – uncertain whether to be negative or affirmative – waits threateningly to be discharged.*(GE)*

Thanks to an absolute regiment, it appears the inventive wealth and the mass of will power are highest and unspent among the Slavs; a German-Slavic ground regiment is thus not the least bit unlikely.*(N)*

---

25 Port Royal (des Champs), founded in 1204 in Versailles, moved to Paris in 1626 by Cistercian nuns, in whose proximity settled more well-known academics (Pascal, among others) and friends of the abbesses, whereby it then became a center for French Catholic scholars.

Sign of the next century – A grandiose goal: the entrance of Russians into culture. Next to barbarism, the awakening of art, the generosity of youth, along with quixotic madness and true will power.[(N)]

We need absolute cooperation with Russia and a *common* plan, in which Russia shall not allow any English schemata within her borders. No American future![(N)]

I love American laughter, especially that of strong sailors like Mark Twain. [(N)]

Beauty, beneath which Americans now understand as stirringly peaceful. To commercial sternness and practical contemplation it is the dry passion of hunting, opposed to victory and reflection.[(N)]

Americans consume too quickly, thus are perhaps only an *apparent* future world power.[(N)]

The Jews are the most remarkable people in the history of the world, because, when confronted with the question of being or not being, they preferred, with a perfectly weird consciousness, being *at any price*: this price was the radical *falsifying* of all nature, of all naturalness, of all actuality, of the entire inner world as well as the outer. They demarcated their position counter to all conditions under which hitherto a people could live, was *permitted* to live; they created out of themselves a concept antithetical to the natural conditions, – they successively reversed, in an irreparable manner, religion, worship, morality, history, and psychology *into the contradiction of their natural values*. We meet with the same phenomenon once more, and in ineffably magnified proportions, although only as a copy: – the Christian Church, in comparison with the "saintly people," dispenses with all pretensions to originality. The Jews, just on that account, are the most *fatal* nation in the history of the world: in their after-effect they made mankind false to such an extent that a Christian can even at present cherish an anti-Jewish feeling without comprehending that he is the *ultimate consequence of Judaism.*[(A)]

The Jews – a people "born for slavery," as Tacitus and the whole ancient world say of them; "the chosen people among the nations," as they themselves say and believe – the Jews performed the miracle of the inversion of valuations, by means of which life on earth obtained a new and dangerous charm for a couple of millenniums. Their prophets fused into one the expressions "rich," "godless," "wicked," "violent," "sensual," and for the first time coined the word "world" as a term of reproach. In this inversion of valuations (in which is also included the use of the word "poor" as synonymous with "saint" and "friend") the significance of the Jewish people is to be found; it is with *them* that the *slave-insurrection in morals* commences.(GE)

All the world's efforts against the "aristocrats," the "mighty," the "masters," the "holders of power," are negligible by comparison with what has been accomplished against those classes by *the Jews* – the Jews, that priestly nation which eventually realized that the one method of effecting satisfaction on its enemies and tyrants was by means of a radical transvaluation of values, which was at the same time an act of the *cleverest revenge.* Yet the method was only appropriate to a nation of priests, to a nation of the most jealously nursed priestly revengefulness. It was the Jews who, in opposition to the aristocratic equation (good = aristocratic = beautiful = happy = loved by the gods), dared with a terrifying logic to suggest the contrary equation, and indeed to maintain with the teeth of the most profound hatred (the hatred of weakness) this contrary equation, namely, "the wretched are alone the good; the poor, the weak, the lowly, are alone the good; the suffering, the needy, the sick, the loathsome, are the only ones who are pious, the only ones who are blessed, for them alone is salvation – but you, on the other hand, you aristocrats, you men of power, you are to all eternity the evil, the horrible, the covetous, the insatiate, the godless; eternally also shall you be the unblessed, the cursed, the damned!" We know who it was who reaped the heritage of this Jewish transvaluation.(GM)

But you understand this not? You have no eyes for a force which has taken two thousand years to achieve victory? – There is nothing wonderful in this: all *lengthy* processes are hard to see and to realize. But *this* is what took place: from the trunk of that tree of revenge and hate, Jewish hate, – that most profound and sublime hate, which creates ideals and changes old values to new creations, the like of which has never been on earth, – there grew a phenomenon which was equally incomparable, *a new love*, the most profound and sublime of all kinds of love; – and from what other trunk could it have grown? But beware of supposing that this love has soared on its upward growth, as in any way a real negation of that thirst for revenge, as an antithesis to the Jewish hate! No, the contrary is the truth! This love grew out of that hate, as its crown, as its triumphant crown, circling wider and wider amid the clarity and fullness of the sun, and pursuing in the very kingdom of light and height its goal of hatred, its victory, its spoil, its strategy, with the same intensity with which the roots of that tree of hate sank into everything which was deep and evil with increasing stability and increasing desire. This Jesus of Nazareth, the incarnate gospel of love, this "Redeemer" bringing salvation and victory to the poor, the sick, the sinful – was he not really temptation in its most sinister and irresistible form, temptation to take the tortuous path to those very *Jewish* values and those very Jewish ideals? Has not Israel really obtained the final goal of its sublime revenge, by the tortuous paths of this "Redeemer," for all that he might pose as Israel's adversary and Israel's destroyer?[(GM)]

The dangers of the Jewish soul are:
1.They gleefully create parasitic settlements.
2.They know how to "adapt," as the naturalists say: through which they have become born actors, like the polyps about which Theognis[26] sang, as they camouflage themselves the color of the cliffs to which they cling.

26 Theognis, Greek poet, * 546 B.C

Their talent, more so the tendency and case of both, appears to be tremendous; adaptation, for the sake of tiny profits, to leave behind most of their spirit and tenacity, has left an ominous furrow in their character: so much so, that even the most respectable dealers within the Jewish money market cannot overcome it, when the circumstances bring with the outstretched, cold blooded hands of petty mesquin[27] greed that would even make a Prussian financier red with shame.[(N)]

If spirit, diligence and ability alone came into consideration, the Prussian Jews will be ready to possess the highest positions of statesman, especially in administrative areas: in short, they would have the "power" *in their hands* (they already have it "in their pockets" as a multitude of evidence has shown). That, of which they are excluded, is their inability to represent power. In their own fatherland, Jews never became the *dominant* caste – their eyes are never convincing, their tongues become twisted after running light and too quickly, their anger understands nothing of the deep, sincere lion's roar, their stomachs hold large feasts, their minds cannot withstand strong wine, their arms and legs allow them no sense of pride (memories are often cultivated in their hands, though I know not which); the manner alone in which a Jew mounts a horse is anything but harmless, and paves way to the understanding that Jews never became a *knightly* race.[(N)]

That Germany has amply *sufficient* Jews, that the German stomach, the German blood, has difficulty (and will long have difficulty) in disposing only of this quantity of "Jew" – as the Italian, the Frenchman, and the Englishman have done by means of a stronger digestion: – that is the unmistakable declaration and language of a general instinct, to which one must listen and according to which one must act. "Let no more Jews come in! And shut the doors, especially towards the East (also towards Austria)!" – thus commands the instinct of a people whose nature is still feeble and uncertain, so that it could be easily wiped out, easily extinguished, by a stronger

27 Mesquin (French) = mean, stingy.

race. The Jews, however, are beyond all doubt the strongest, toughest, and purest race at present living in Europe; they know how to succeed even under the worst conditions (in fact, better than under favorable ones), by means of virtues of some sort, which one would like nowadays to label as vices – owing above all to a resolute faith which does not need to be ashamed before "modern ideas"; they alter only, *when* they do alter, in the same way that the Russian Empire makes its conquest – as an empire that has plenty of time and is not of yesterday – namely, according to the principle, "as slowly as possible"! A thinker who has the future of Europe at heart, will, in all his perspectives concerning the future, calculate upon the Jews, as he will calculate upon the Russians, as above all the surest and likeliest factors in the great play and battle of forces.[GE]

Amid the dramas to which the upcoming century invites us, one is the decision regarding the destiny of the European Jews. The fact that their die is cast and they have crossed the point of no return is now tangibly obvious: all that is left for them is to either become the masters of Europe or to lose Europe as they lost Egypt long ago, where they placed themselves between a similar either-or.[D]

II

Time's Frailty

Zeitgeist

On Passing-By

Thus slowly wandering through many peoples and divers cities, did Zarathustra return by round-about roads to his mountains and his cave.

And behold, thereby came he unawares also to the gate of the *great* city. Here, however, a foaming fool, with extended hands, sprang forward to him and stood in his way. It was the same fool whom the people called "the ape of Zarathustra": for he had learned from him something of the expression and modulation of language, and perhaps liked also to borrow from the store of his wisdom. And the fool talked thus to Zarathustra:

O Zarathustra, here is the great city: here hast thou nothing to seek and everything to lose.

Why wouldst thou wade through this mire? Have pity upon thy foot! Spit rather on the gate of the city, and – turn back!

Here is the hell for anchorites' thoughts: here are great thoughts seethed alive and boiled small.

Here do all great sentiments decay: here may only rattle-boned sensations rattle!

Smellest thou not already the shambles and cookshops of the spirit? Steameth not this city with the fumes of slaughtered spirit?

Seest thou not the souls hanging like limp dirty rags? – And they make newspapers also out of these rags!

Hearest thou not how spirit hath here become a verbal game? Loathsome verbal swill doth it vomit forth! – And they make newspapers also out of this verbal swill.

They hound one another, and know not whither! They inflame one another, and know not why! They tinkle with their pinchbeck, they jingle with their gold.

They are cold, and seek warmth from distilled waters: they are inflamed, and seek coolness from frozen spirits; they are all sick and sore through public opinion.

All lusts and vices are here at home; but here there are also the virtuous; there is much appointable appointed virtue: –

Much appointable virtue with scribe-fingers, and hardy sitting-flesh and waiting-flesh, blessed with small breast-stars, and padded, haunchless daughters.

There is here also much piety, and much faithful spittle-licking and spittle-backing, before the God of Hosts.

"From on high," drippeth the star, and the gracious spittle; for the high, longeth every starless bosom.

The moon hath its court, and the court hath its moon-calves: unto all, however, that cometh from the court do the mendicant people pray, and all appointable mendicant virtues.

"I serve, thou servest, we serve" – so prayeth all appointable virtue to the prince: that the merited star may at last stick on the slender breast!

But the moon still revolveth around all that is earthly: so

revolveth also the prince around what is earthliest of all – that, however, is the gold of the shopman.

The God of the Hosts of war is not the God of the golden bar; the prince proposeth, but the shopman – disposeth!

By all that is luminous and strong and good in thee, O Zarathustra! Spit on this city of shopmen and return back!

Here floweth all blood putridly and tepidly and frothily through all veins: spit on the great city, which is the great slum where all the scum frotheth together!

Spit on the city of compressed souls and slender breasts, of pointed eyes and sticky fingers –

– On the city of the obtrusive, the brazen-faced, the pen-demagogues and tongue-demagogues, the overheated ambitious:
– Where everything maimed, ill-famed, lustful, untrustful, over-mellow, sickly-yellow and seditious, festereth perniciously: –

– Spit on the great city and turn back! –

Here, however, did Zarathustra interrupt the foaming fool, and shut his mouth.

– Stop this at once! called out Zarathustra, long have thy speech and thy species disgusted me!

Why didst thou live so long by the swamp, that thou thyself hadst to become a frog and a toad?

Floweth there not a tainted, frothy, swamp-blood in thine own veins, when thou hast thus learned to croak and revile?

Why wentest thou not into the forest? Or why didst thou not till the ground? Is the sea not full of green islands?

I despise thy contempt; and when thou warnedst me – why didst thou not warn thyself?

Out of love alone shall my contempt and my warning bird take wing; but not out of the swamp! –

They call thee mine ape, thou foaming fool: but I call thee my grunting-pig, – by thy grunting, thou spoilest even my praise of folly.

What was it that first made thee grunt? Because no one sufficiently *flattered* thee: – therefore didst thou seat thyself beside this filth, that thou mightest have cause for much grunting, –

– That thou mightest have cause for much *vengeance*! For vengeance, thou vain fool, is all thy foaming; I have divined thee well!

But thy fools'-word injureth *me*, even when thou art right! And even if Zarathustra's word *were* a hundred times justified, thou wouldst ever – *do* wrong with my word!

Thus spake Zarathustra. Then did he look on the great city and sighed, and was long silent. At last he spake thus:

I loathe also this great city, and not only this fool. Here and there – there is nothing to better, nothing to worsen.

Woe to this great city! – And I would that I already saw the pillar of fire in which it will be consumed!

For such pillars of fire must precede the great noontide. But this hath its time and its own fate. –

This precept, however, give I unto thee, in parting, thou fool:

Where one can no longer love, there should one – *pass by!* –

Thus spake Zarathustra, and passed by the fool and the great city. [(Z)]

Our era is known by everyone as an era of transition, and they are right. However, not because this concept belongs to our era more than it does any other. Anywhere else we have settled throughout history we found unrest, old concepts locked in battle with the new, and people, who were once called prophets, living fragile lifestyles, entrenched in their own experiences, who knew this, and therefore lived in constant fear. This is how it happens – everything crumbles, and so the world falls. But it is not irrevocably fallen –the old roots of the forest wither, but a new forest always grows back: in every era there is both a rotting and emerging world. [(N)]

Our age gives the impression of an interim state; the old-world views and old cultures linger among us, while the new, not yet secure in routine, thus lack decision and consistency. It appears as though everything is turning to chaos with the old fading away and the new becoming useless and weaker. But so it is with the soldier learning to march: for a time he is as insecure and awkward as ever because at first his muscles move according to the old system then must adapt to the new, and neither has yet claimed victory. We are in flux, but we need not let it infect us with fear and sacrifice all we have earned. Furthermore, we *cannot* step back to the old, we *have* burned our ships; all that remains is our bravery. Come what may. [(H)]

The Chinese have a proverb which mothers even teach their children: "*Siao-sin*" (*"make thy heart small"*). This is the essentially fundamental tendency in latter-day civilizations. I have no doubt that an ancient Greek, also, would first of all remark the self-dwarfing in us Europeans of today – in this respect alone we should immediately be "distasteful" to him.[(GE)]

I believe everything we Europeans of today habitually admire as the values of all these revered things called "humanity," "mankind," "sympathy," "pity," may hold some value as the weakening and mitigation of certain powerful, dangerous primal instincts. In the long run all these things are nevertheless nothing other than the lessening of "man" entirely, and his *mediocritizing* – to such a desperate situation I will refer to with a desperate expression. I believe the comedia umana[28] for an Epicurean[29] spectator god must consist of this: that the Europeans, by virtue of their growing morality, believe in all their innocence and vanity that they are rising higher, but truly they are *sinking* – meaning, through the cultivation of all virtues which are useful to a herd, and through the repression of contrary virtues which bear a new, higher, stronger, *masterful type* of man, merely develop the herd-animal in man... [(N)]

If one could observe the strangely painful, equally coarse and refined comedy of European Christianity with the derisive and impartial eye of an Epicurean god, I should think one would never cease marveling and laughing; does it not actually seem that some single will has ruled over Europe for eighteen centuries in order to make a *sublime abortion* of man? He, however, who, with opposite requirements (no longer Epicurean) and with some divine hammer in his hand, could approach this almost voluntary degeneration and stunting of mankind, as exemplified in the European Christian (Pascal, for instance), would he not have to cry aloud with rage, pity, and horror: "Oh, you bunglers, presumptuous pitiful bunglers, what have you done! Was that a work for your hands? How have you hacked and botched my finest stone! What have *you* presumed to do!" – I should say that Christianity has hitherto been the most portentous of presumptions. Men, not great enough, nor hard enough, to be entitled as artists to take part in fashioning *man*; men, not sufficiently strong and far-sighted to *allow*, with sublime self-constraint, the obvious law of the thousandfold

28 Comedia Umana = humane comedy.

29 Epicurean, derived from the Greek philosopher Epicurus, * 270 B.C. Here = entirely peaceful, stoic. For Epicurus taught that the greatest joy, in a well-balanced soul's peace, exists in the invincibility of the mind.

failures and perishing to prevail; men, not sufficiently noble to see the radically different grades of rank and intervals of rank that separate man from man: – *such* men, with their "equality before God," have hitherto swayed the destiny of Europe; until at last a dwarfed, almost ludicrous species has been produced, a gregarious animal, something obliging, sickly, mediocre, the European of the present day.*(GE)*

In Europe morality is that of herd animals – thus, *one* type of morality, next to which many other possibilities have long existed and still do. However, for the last two centuries in Europe, with the help of a herd animal religion, the effort was put forth using thorough methods to bring all instincts of the herd animal under control: we have not completely satisfied its apparent and recent manifestation with democratic institutions, along with its desires and hopes of the similar instincts, as the wailing of every socialist proves: firstly, socialism is the well thought out herd animal morality: namely with the proposition "equal justice for all," which leaps to the conclusions "equal entitlements for all," "a herd without a shepherd," "sheep equally sheep," "peace on earth," and "all people will gleefully stand beside one another." *(N)*

The domestication of men has become commonplace in this democratic Europe. Men, who learn easily, and easily toe the line, are the rule: the herd animal, though highly intelligent, is groomed thusly.*(N)*

Do you want life to be easy? Then remain with the herd and forget about ever rising above the herd. *(N)*

The tendency of the herd is geared toward deadlock and preservation. Nothing creative lies therein.*(N)*

Let us at once say again what we have already said a hundred times, for people's ears nowadays are unwilling to hear such truths – *our* truths. We know well enough how offensively it sounds when any one plainly, and without metaphor, counts man amongst the animals; but it will be accounted to us almost a *crime*, that it is precisely in respect to men of "modern ideas" that we have constantly applied the terms "herd," "herd-instincts," and such like expressions. What avail is it? We cannot do otherwise, for it is precisely here that our new insight is. We have found that in all the principal moral judgments Europe has become unanimous, including likewise the countries where European influence prevails: in Europe people evidently *know* what Socrates thought he did not know, and what the famous serpent of old once promised to teach – they "know" today what is good and evil. It must then sound hard and be distasteful to the ear, when we always insist that that which here thinks it knows, that which here glorifies itself with praise and blame, and calls itself good, is the instinct of the herding human animal: the instinct which has come and is ever coming more and more to the front, to preponderance and supremacy over other instincts, according to the increasing physiological approximation and resemblance of which it is the symptom. *Morality in Europe at present is herding-animal morality;* and therefore, as we understand the matter, only one kind of human morality, beside which, before which, and after which many other moralities, and above all *higher* moralities, are or should be possible. Against such a "possibility," against such a "should be," however, this morality defends itself with all its strength; it says obstinately and inexorably: "I am morality itself and nothing else is morality!" Indeed, with the help of a religion which has humored and flattered the sublimest desires of the herding-animal, things have reached such a point that we always find a more visible expression of this morality even in political and social arrangements: the *democratic* movement is the inheritance of the Christian movement.[(GE)]

Legislative moralities are the principal means by which one can form mankind, according to the fancy of a creative and profound will: provided of course, that such an artistic will of the first order gets the power into its own hands, and can make its creative will prevail over long periods in the form of legislation, religions and morals. At present, and probably for some time to come, one will seek such colossally creative men, such really great men, as I understand them, in vain: they will be lacking, until, after many disappointments, we are forced to begin to understand why it is they are lacking, and that nothing bars with greater hostility their rise and development, at present and for some time to come, than that which is now called *the* morality in Europe. Just as if there were no other kind of morality, and could be no other kind, than the one we have already characterised as herd-morality. It is this morality which is now striving with all its power to attain to that green-meadow happiness on earth, which consists in security, absence of danger, ease, facilities for livelihood, and, last but not least, "if all goes well," even hopes to dispense with all kinds of shepherds and bell-wethers.[(WP)]

Whoever examines the conscience of the present-day European, will always elicit the same imperative from its thousand moral folds and hidden recesses, the imperative of the timidity of the herd: "we wish that some time or other there may be *nothing more to fear!*" Some time or other – the will and the way *thereto* is nowadays called "progress" all over Europe.[(GE)]

Progress. Let us be on our guard lest we deceive ourselves! Time flies forward apace – we would fain believe that everything flies forward with it – that evolution is an advancing development... That is the appearance of things which deceives the most circumspect. But the nineteenth century shows no advance whatever on the sixteenth: and the German spirit of 1888 is an example of a backward movement when compared with that of 1788... [(WP)]

The belief in "progress"– in lower spheres of intelligence, appears as increasing life: but this is self-deception: in higher spheres of intelligence it is a sign of *declining* life. [(WP)]

O thou too proud European of the nineteenth century, art thou not mad? Thy knowledge does not complete Nature, it only kills thine own nature! Measure the height of what thou knowest by the depths of thy power to *do*. Thou climbest the sunbeams of knowledge up towards heaven – but also down to Chaos. Thy manner of going is fatal to thee; the ground slips from under thy feet into the unknown; thy life has no other stay, but only spider's webs that every new stroke of thy knowledge tears asunder. [(UM)]

It is dire to contemplate, whether there remains a basis for for a culture that is yet to become.[(N)]

The whole of our culture in Europe has long been writhing in agony of suspense which increases from decade to decade as if in expectation of a catastrophe: restless, violent, helter-skelter, like a torrent that will *reach its bourne*, and refuses to reflect – yea, that even dreads reflection.[(WP)]

There is nothing from which our civilization suffers *more* than from the superfluity of presumptuous hodmen and fragmental humanities; our universities are, against their will, the real forcing houses for this mode of stunted growth of intellectual instincts.[(T)]

Danger of our culture. We belong to an age whose culture is in danger of collapsing through the very means of attaining culture. [(H)]

I shall only give two instances showing how utterly the sentiment of our time has been perverted, and how completely unconscious the present age is of this perversion. Formerly financiers were looked down upon with honest scorn, even though they were recognized as needful; for it was generally admitted that every society must have its viscera. Now, however, they are the ruling power in the soul of modern humanity, for they constitute the most covetous portion thereof. In former times people were warned especially against taking the day or the moment too seriously: the *nil admirari*[30] was recommended and the care of

30 Nil Admirari (Latin) = to wonder about nothing (beginning of a poem by Horace).

things eternal. Now there is but one kind of seriousness left in the modern mind, and it is limited to the news brought by the newspaper and the telegraph. Improve each shining hour, turn it to some account and judge it as quickly as possible! – one would think modern men had but one virtue left – presence of mind. Unfortunately, it much more closely resembles the omnipresence of disgusting and insatiable cupidity, and spying inquisitiveness become universal. For the question is whether *mind is present at all today*; – but we shall leave this problem for future judges to solve; they, at least, are bound to pass modern men through a sieve. But that this age is vulgar, even we can see now, and it is so because it reveres precisely what nobler ages contemned. If, therefore, it loots all the treasures of bygone wit and wisdom, and struts about in this richest of rich garments, it only proves its sinister consciousness of its own vulgarity in so doing; for it does not don this garb for warmth, but merely in order to mystify its surroundings.[(UM)]

Era of comparison. The less men are bound by tradition, the greater the motivations within them stir, and consequently greater is their outward restlessness, their moving around together, and the polyphony of their deeds. Who now still feels a strong urge to bind himself and his succession to a specific place? Who still feels any strong attachment at all? As it is with art, all the genres are reproduced side by side, so are all the stepping stones and genres of morality, custom and culture.[(H)]

The man of an age of dissolution which mixes the races with one another, who has the inheritance of a diversified descent in his body – that is to say, contrary, and often not only contrary, instincts and standards of value, which struggle with one another and are seldom at peace – such a man of late culture and broken lights, will, on an average, be a weak man.[(GE)]

The era of great happenings will be, despite all even the pettiest of eras brought forth, when people are extremely flexible, and made of rubber.[(N)]

Our era is agitated, and in no way an era of passion; it heats itself constantly because it does not feel warmth – it essentially freezes itself. I do not believe in the greatness of these "great happenings" of which people speak.*(N)*

Our agitated era pretends that an eternal tumultuousness and imbalance of atmosphere characterizes the greatest men: it knows nothing of the consistent, deep, powerful currents that flow with purpose: it makes waves, cries out, and feels not the pitifulness of this erratic agitation. *(N)*

What, to you, is "experience?" How a swarm of mosquitoes descends upon you, your skin will be bitten all over, but your heart will know nothing of it.*(N)*

"I do not know out or in; I am whatever does not know out or in" – sighs modern man... We were ill from *that* modernism, – from lazy peace, from cowardly compromise, from the whole virtuous uncleanness of modern yea and nay. That tolerance and *largeur*[31] of heart which "forgives" all because it "understands" all, is Sirocco to us. Better to live in the ice than among modern virtues and other south-winds!*(A)*

The modern man suffers from a weakened personality. The Roman of the Empire ceased to be a Roman through the contemplation of the world that lay at his feet; he lost himself in the crowd of foreigners that streamed into Rome, and degenerated amid the cosmopolitan carnival of arts, worships and moralities. It is the same with the modern man, who is continually having a world-panorama unrolled before his eyes by his historical artists. He is turned into a restless, dilettante spectator, and arrives at a condition when even great wars and revolutions cannot affect him beyond the moment.*(UM)*

By its lofty ideal, Christianity has outbidden the ancient Systems of Ethics and their invariable naturalism, with which men came

31 Largeur (French) = width, breadth.

to feel a dull disgust: and afterwards when they did reach the knowledge of what was better and higher, they found they had no longer the power, for all their desire, to return to its embodiment in the antique virtues. And so the life of the modern man is passed in see-sawing between Christianity and Paganism, between a furtive or hypocritical approach to Christian morality, and an equally shy and spiritless dallying with the antique: and he does not thrive under it. His inherited fear of naturalism and its more recent attraction for him, his desire to come to rest somewhere, while in the impotence of his intellect he swings backwards and forwards between the "good" and the "better" course – all this argues an instability in the modern mind that condemns it to be without joy or fruit.*(UM)*

Regarded merely as a spectacle, and compared with other and earlier manifestations of human life, the existence of modern man is characterized by indescribable indigence and exhaustion, despite the unspeakable garishness at which only the superficial observer rejoices. If one examines a little more closely the impression which this vehement and kaleidoscopic play of colors makes upon one, does not the whole seem to blaze with the shimmer and sparkle of innumerable little stones borrowed from former civilizations? Is not everything one sees merely a complex of inharmonious bombast, aped gesticulations, arrogant superficiality? – a ragged suit of motley for the naked and the shivering? A seeming dance of joy enjoined upon a sufferer? Aris of overbearing pride assumed by one who is sick to the backbone? And the whole moving with such rapidity and confusion that it is disguised and masked – sordid impotence, devouring dissension, assiduous ennui, dishonest distress!*(UM)*

It may be one-sided, to insist only on the blurred lines and the dull colors in the picture of modern life: yet the other side is no more encouraging, it is only more disturbing. There is certainly strength there, enormous strength; but it is wild, primitive and merciless. One looks on with a chill expectancy, as though into the caldron of a witch's kitchen; every moment there may arise sparks and vapor, to herald some fearful apparition. For a century we have been ready for a world-shaking convulsion; and though we have lately been trying to set the conservative strength of the so-called national state against the great modern tendency to volcanic destructiveness, it will only be, for a long time yet, an aggravation of the universal unrest that hangs over us. We need not be deceived by individuals behaving as if they knew nothing of all this anxiety: their own restlessness shows how well they know it. They think more exclusively of themselves than men ever thought before; they plant and build for their little day, and the chase for happiness is never greater than when the quarry must be caught today or tomorrow: the next day perhaps there is no more hunting. We live in the Atomic Age, or rather in the Atomic Chaos. [(UM)]

Nihilism stands at the gate: wherefrom does this most ghastly guest visit us? Starting point: the *cause* of nihilism is indicated by an error of "social emergencies," "physiological degradations," or due entirely to corruption... These emergencies allow perpetually varying interpretations. But also: via a *completely accurate interpretation*, such as Christian morality, nihilism fades away.[(N)]

What does nihilism mean? *The highest values void themselves.* Direction is missing; the answer to the "why?" is missing.[(N)]

Modern pessimism is an expression of the uselessness only of the *modern* world, not of the world and existence as such.[(WP)]

Criticism of modernism. – Our institutions are no longer worth anything: that is a matter on which we are unanimous. But the fault is not in the institutions, but in *us*. After we have lost all instincts out of which institutions grow, the institutions themselves are being lost, because *we* are no longer suitable for them. Democratism has always been the *décadence* type of organizing power... [(T)]

Democracy is *the natural consequence* of Christianity.[(N)]

Europe is a collapsing world. Democracy is the *decaying form* of the state. [(N)]

European democracy is, to the smallest degree, the unleashing of forces. Above all, it is an unleashing of laziness, weariness, *weakness*.[(N)]

Disregard for, along with the decline and *death of the state*, the unleashing of the private person … is the consequence of the conceptualized democratic state... [(H)]

The people who were worth something, who *became* worth something, never acquired their greatness under liberal institutions... [(T)]

Liberal institutions immediately cease to be liberal, as soon as they are attained; afterwards, there are no more mischievous or more radical enemies of freedom than liberal institutions. One knows well enough *what* they accomplish: they undermine the will to power, they are the levelling of mountain and valley exalted into morality, they make people small, cowardly, and voluptuous, – with them the herding animal always triumphs. Liberalism: that is *increased herding-animality.*[(T)]

Democracy represents the disbelief in great men and elite society: "One man is equal to the next." "Fundamentally we are all self-serving cattle and rabble." [(N)]

Equal justice for all – that is the outstanding injustice; for the highest men arrive too soon.[(N)]

The doctrine of equality! … But there exists no deadlier poison; for it *seems* to be preached by justice itself, while it *does away* with justice...[(T)]

"Equality," as an actual approximation to similarity, of which the theory of "equal rights" is but the expression, belongs essentially to *décadence*: the gap between man and man, between class and class, the multiplicity of types, the will to assert itself, to stand out in contrast, that which I call *pathos of distance* belongs to every *vigorous* period. [(T)]

This age is possessed of the *opposite* instincts. What it wants, above all, is comfort; secondly, it wants publicity and the deafening din of actors' voices, the big drum which appeals to its Bank Holiday tastes; thirdly, that every one should lie on his belly in utter subjection before the greatest of all lies – which is "the equality of men" – and should honor only those virtues which *make men equal and place them in equal positions*.[(WP)]

Difference prevails among the smallest of things, such as sperm, and eggs – equality is an extraordinary delusion. [(N)]

The general *oversimplification* of the European soul, a certain awkward uncertainty, which happily prides itself as having a tune of straightforwardness, honesty or scientific character: that is the force of the democratic Zeitgeist and its musty air: moreover, it is the force of the newspaper readers.[(N)]

The Press. Let us consider how, even today, all great political events sneak silently behind the curtain, how they are concealed by trivial events and appear minor next to them, how it is long after they have occurred that their dire effects are felt as the ground shakes – with the press as it now is, with its daily wave of hot air spreading dread, exclaiming, inciting, alarming, what meaning can we now give it – is it something more than a *perpetual false alarm* that leads the ears and senses down the wrong path? [(H)]

We now face the repercussions of the "great" happenings – the repercussions of the press. [(N)]

The power of the press remains because each individual who serves it feels no sense of responsibility or duty. He casually expresses *his* opinion, but sometimes *not*, only to serve his party, the politics of his country, or finally himself. Such small lapses of dishonesty, or perhaps a mere dishonest secrecy, are not hard for the individual to bear, but their consequences are enormous because these small lapses of many occur simultaneously. Each of them says to himself: "For such lowly services, I shall have my livelihood; to refuse such small acts of discretion would make it impossible." Because it seems well-nigh a matter of moral indifference whether one writes a single line, more lines, fails to write it, perhaps moreover without one's name being on it, anyone with money and influence can turn any opinion into public opinion. Whoever knows that most people are weak in small matters, and desires to reach his goal using them as means, is always a dangerous man.[*(H)*]

The freedom of the press ruins style, and ultimately spirit.[*(N)*]

I am against parliamentarianism and the press, for they are the means with which the herd animal believes it turns itself into a god.[*(N)*]

Parliaments can be highly useful to a strong and pragmatic statesman: there he has something to rely on... on which he can place a great amount of responsibility. Altogether, however, I wish the increasing nonsense and superstitious faith in majorities were not established in Germany, as with the Latin races, and that something new could finally be invented, even in politics! It is senseless and dangerous to let the custom of universal suffrage, which is still young enough to be easily swept away, take a deeper root: while of course, its introduction was a mere momentary measure to keep away from contemporary difficulties.[*(N)*]

The Old and the Young. "There is something immoral about parliaments" – many continue to think – "because there, one is also allowed to hold views contrary to those of the government!"

– "One must always hold the view of whatever is commanded by our sovereign lord" – this is the Eleventh Commandment in many an honest aged head, especially in northern Germany. One laughs about it like it is old fashioned: but at that time it was morality! Perhaps one day, amid the younger generation raised in parliamentary institutions, there will be laughter at that which now stands as moral: namely, to place the policy of the party above one's own wisdom and to answer every question of public welfare in a way that will blow a favorable wind for the party's sails. "One must hold the view of whatever is demanded by the situation of the party" – and so the canon of conduct would sound. In service to this kind of morality, men are now prepared for every kind of sacrifice, self-conquest and martyrdom.*(D)*

Nowadays, when the state has a nonsensically oversized belly, in all fields and branches of work there are "representatives" over and above the real workman: for instance, in addition to the scholars, there are the journalists; in addition to the suffering masses, there is a crowd of jabbering and bragging ne'er-do-wells who "represent" that suffering – not to speak of the professional politicians who, though quite satisfied with their lot, stand up in Parliament and, with strong lungs, "represent" grievances. Our modern life is extremely *expensive*, thanks the host of middlemen that infest it; whereas in the city of antiquity, and in many a city of Spain and Italy today, where there is an echo of the ancient spirit, the man himself comes forward and will have nothing to do with a representative or an intermediary in the modern style – except perhaps to kick him hence! *(WP)*

The educated complain about the crowd and its lack of discipline; if this were proven, contempt would fall hard upon the educated; the crowd is no better nor more evil than the educated. The crowd displays its vile dissolution while the educated display their lack of discipline. A man may take the reins, become their leader and live as he wants; and he will either uplift or ruin them, after he has either uplifted or ruined himself.*(N)*

The masses seem to be worth notice in three aspects only: first as the copies of great men, printed on bad paper from worn-out plates, next as a contrast to the great men, and lastly as their tools: for the rest, let the devil and statistics fly away with them! *(UM)*

How does one best address the masses? *I do not know.* It has nothing to do with my work. It seems to me, that one must make life very *difficult* through demands of strict virtues: otherwise people become lazy and useless, in both body and mind. *(N)*

What produces today our repulsion towards "man"? – for we *suffer* from "man," there is no doubt about it. It is not fear; it is rather that we have nothing more to fear from men; it is that the worm "man" is in the foreground and pullulates; it is that the "tame man," the wretched mediocre and unedifying creature, has learnt to consider himself a goal and a pinnacle, an inner meaning, an historic principle, a "higher man." *(GM)*

Generation

The Land of Culture

Too far did I fly into the future: a horror seized upon me.

And when I looked around me, lo! there time was my sole contemporary.

Then did I fly backwards, homewards – and always faster. Thus did I come unto you: ye present-day men, and into the land of culture.

For the first time brought I an eye to see you, and good desire: verily, with longing in my heart did I come.

But how did it turn out with me? Although so alarmed – I had yet to laugh! Never did mine eye see anything so motley-colored!

I laughed and laughed, while my foot still trembled, and my heart as well. “Here forsooth, is the home of all the paintpots,” – said I.

With fifty patches painted on faces and limbs – so sat ye there to mine astonishment, ye present-day men!

And with fifty mirrors around you, which flattered your play of colors, and repeated it!

Verily, ye could wear no better masks, ye present-day men, than your own faces! Who could – *recognize* you!

Written all over with the characters of the past, and these characters also pencilled over with new characters – thus have ye concealed yourselves well from all decipherers!

And though one be a trier of the reins, who still believeth that ye have reins! Out of colors ye seem to be baked, and out of glued scraps.

Time's Frailty

All times and peoples gaze divers-colored out of your veils; all customs and beliefs speak divers-colored out of your gestures.

He who would strip you of veils and wrappers, and paints and gestures, would just have enough left to scare the crows.

Verily, I myself am the scared crow that once saw you naked, and without paint; and I flew away when the skeleton ogled at me.

Rather would I be a day-laborer in the nether-world, and among the shades of the by-gone! – Fatter and fuller than ye, are forsooth the netherworldlings!

This, yea this, is bitterness to my bowels, that I can neither endure you naked nor clothed, ye present-day men!

All that is unhomelike in the future, and whatever maketh strayed birds shiver, is verily more homelike and familiar than your "reality."

For thus speak ye: "Real are we wholly, and without faith and Superstition": thus do ye plume yourselves – alas! even without plumes!

Indeed, how would ye be *able* to believe, ye divers-colored ones! – ye who are pictures of all that hath ever been believed!

Perambulating refutations are ye, of belief itself, and a dislocation of all thought. *Untrustworthy ones*: thus do I call you, ye real ones!

All periods prate against one another in your spirits; and the dreams and pratings of all periods were even realer than your wakefulness!

Unfruitful are ye: *therefore* do ye lack belief. But he who had to create, had always his presaging dreams and astral premonitions

– and believed in believing! –

Half-open doors are ye, at which grave-diggers wait. And this is *your* reality: "Everything deserveth to perish."

Alas, how ye stand there before me, ye unfruitful ones; how lean your ribs! And many of you surely have had knowledge thereof.

Many a one hath said: "There hath surely a God filched something from me secretly whilst I slept? Verily, enough to make a girl for himself therefrom!

"Amazing is the poverty of my ribs!" thus hath spoken many a present-day man.

Yea, ye are laughable unto me, ye present-day men! And especially when ye marvel at yourselves!

And woe unto me if I could not laugh at your marvelling, and had to swallow all that is repugnant in your platters!

As it is, however, I will make lighter of you, since I have to carry *what is heavy*; and what matter if beetles and May-bugs also alight on my load!

Verily, it shall not on that account become heavier to me! And not from you, ye present-day men, shall my great weariness arise. –

Ah, whither shall I now ascend with my longing! From all mountains do I look out for fatherlands and motherlands.

But a home have I found nowhere: unsettled am I in all cities, and decamping at all gates.

Alien to me, and a mockery, are the present-day men, to whom of late my heart impelled me; and exiled am I from fatherlands and motherlands.

Thus do I love only my *children's land*, the undiscovered in the remotest sea: for it do I bid my sails search and search.

Unto my children will I make amends for being the child of my fathers: and unto all the future – for *this* present-day! – Thus spake Zarathustra.[(Z)]

"I wish to hide nothing from you, my professor," so states... his assistant. "For too long am I at your side, listening all too attentively, in order to fully devote myself to our current education system. I feel every tangible hopeless mistake and grievance all too deeply – and yet, any power I could wield via valiant struggle that would get results I see little of in myself. An overall despondency has befallen me; the flight into solitude was neither arrogance, nor pretentiousness. I will happily describe for you the signature I discovered inscribed within the lively and hastily moving educational issues. Apparently I must decide between two principle directions – they are two apparent opposites, both ephemeral in their work, their results bear long awaited confluent currents that control the present educational institutions: the drive toward the furthest possible *expansion and propagation* of education, along with the drive toward *diminishing and weakening* of education itself. In one direction, and for various reasons, education should impregnate the broadest circles as demanded by tendency. The other direction should be expected to oppose education, give up the highest, noblest, and most sublime aspirations, and humbly place itself into the service of a life form such as the state.

"I trust I have heard which side of the call for aggressive expansion and propagation of education rings with the most clarity. This expansion includes the beloved national economical dogmas of today. The more knowledge and education there is, the more production and need there will be, therefore greater happiness – so hypothesizes the formula. Here we have the utilization as the goal, purpose and more accurately the acquisition of education striving for the largest possible profit. Education will be roughly defined via this direction as the insight, with which one can place himself 'upon the heights of his time,' find all paths that will make the most money with ease, and gain control of every resource flowing between peoples and states. The true educational task will consequently fabricate as many 'kurante'[32] men as possible, 'kurant' in the same vain as a coin. The more such 'kurante' men exist the happier a people will be: now, this must be the purpose of the modern educational institute – to further each student to become as 'kurant' as his nature will allow, to build each one based on this type, that he, from his own degree of knowledge and wisdom, attains the maximum amount of happiness and gain. Each student must be able to accurately gauge himself, as he must know how much he has to gain in life. To profess the views of the 'federation of intelligence and possession,' is virtually a moral requisite. Each type of education that causes loneliness, flaunts its aspirations regarding money and acquisition and consumes time is despised: the student is careful enough to dismiss any other educational tendencies as 'higher egoism' and 'immoral Epicurean education.'[33] After the prevailing morality, an opposite will naturally be necessary, namely a *swift* education in order to swiftly create something that generates profit, and yet a thorough education in order to create something that can generate an *extraordinary* amount of profit. To a man only so much culture can act in the interests of acquisition, but so much will be demanded of him. Essentially, it is necessary for mankind to stake a claim to happiness on earth, and only therefore is education necessary!"

The assistant speaks further: "there are other motives behind the bravely pursued expansion and propagation of education beyond the lingering national economical dogma. The fear of religious oppression is prevalent in a few countries, and the dread of its aftermath is so pronounced, it is felt in every social class of education with longing desires and elements that have

32 Kurant (French, courant) = passable, practical.

33 Epicurean Education (Epicureanism, named after the Greek philosopher Epicurus, the teacher of pleasureful enjoyment of life) last but not least a connoisseur of learning to will for oneself.

been sucked dry via the eradication religious instincts have long enforced. Elsewhere, for its part, the state strives for its own survival and desires the furthest possible expansion of education because it desires the ability to withhold even the strongest unleashing of education within its yoke, for which it knows it's able, and it has been proven that whether extended education benefits its officials or its armies, the state itself always benefits from competition with other states. In this case, the foundation of the state must be solid and vast in order to balance the complicated educational arch, just as in the first case the traces of prior religious oppression must remain tangible enough in order to sell a desperate remedy. Thus, the provocation of people's war cries demanding more national education must be carefully differentiated in order to decipher whether a lush tendency towards acquisition and possession, stigmas of an early religious oppression, or the clever ego of a state provoked this war cry.

"In contrast it seems to me, though it was not that loud, it was at least insistently provoked from different sides by another drive, the drive toward the *diminishing of education.*

"The student grooms himself in accordance with this drive as it is whispered in his ear in all scholarly circles: the overbearing fact, that with today's desired utilization of scholars in the service of their science, the *education* of scholars will become more arbitrary and incidental. For within a wide breadth scientific studies are so broad, that the student, with merely satisfactory assets and a desire to accomplish anything, will operate in a particular field and thereby recklessly leave all else behind. He must stand above the crowd in his field, otherwise they own him. Such an exclusive specialist is similar to the factory worker who, for his entire life has done nothing other than turn a certain screw or flip a specific lever, work with a particular tool or machine, wherein he indeed attains unbelievable virtuosity. In Germany, this narrow professionalism of our scholars is so astoundingly admired that such painful facts are worn like a glorious cloak, and their further waywardness from proper education is seen as a moral phenomenon: the 'loyalty of the few,' the 'loyalty of the cart drivers,' the pageant theme of illiteracy beyond the field will be signs of the show's modesty.

"Throughout the centuries it has become self-evident that educated scholars are only comprehended by other scholars; the experience of our time would direly prompt a naïve equality. For now the accepted condition is the exploitation of man's favor of science without any decency: who would probe further as to what gives science such value that allows it to consume its subjects like a vampire? The division of labor in science strives towards a similar goal, after religions strive toward consciousness, after a diminishing of education, and naturally after the destruction of the same kind. A few religions, in accordance with their genesis and history, and with a justifiable desire, can at some point offer a self-immolation for science. Now we are prepared for the point where all general questions of genuine nature, before all the highest philosophical problems of the scientific man, lose their chance to preach: whereas that sticky binding layer that has worked itself between the sciences, known as journalism, has a task to fulfill here, which is to conduct itself in accordance with its essence, as the meaning its name holds, as a daily labor.

"In journalism namely, both directions work side by side: expansion and diminishing of education shake hands; the magazine essentially steps on the toes of education, and the scholar mandates educational requirements, remains entrenched in that sticky network layer that is grouted in the joints of every life form, rank, art, science, and is just as firm and fail safe as the magazine appears to be. The more peculiar educational goal of the present is culminated within the magazine: how equally the journalist, as a servant to the moment, at the place of great genius, as the leader of all time and the savior from the moment, is trampled upon. Now tell me, my most excellent master, what should I do for my hopes in the struggle against this achieved reversal of every true educational aspiration? How can I, as an individual, face it with courage and then allow it to occur, even though I know it in my heart, that every scattered seed of true education will be mercilessly crushed beneath the wheel of this pseudo education?

"Think about how fruitless the intense work of the teacher must be, when one student submerges himself in the vast distance of the cryptic Hellenic world and wishes to incorporate it within the true education of his homeland: then an hour later the same student reaches for a newspaper, period novel, or a picture book, whose stylistics bear the disgusting coat of arms of barbaric modern education." *(N)*

If, however, our public and private life is so manifestly devoid of all signs of a productive and characteristic culture; if, moreover, our great artists, with that earnest vehemence and honesty which is peculiar to greatness admit, and have admitted, this monstrous fact – so very humiliating to a gifted nation; how can it still be possible for contentment to reign to such an astonishing extent among German scholars? And since the last war this complacent spirit has seemed ever more and more ready to break forth into exultant cries and demonstrations of triumph. At all events, the belief seems to be rife that we are in possession of a genuine culture, and the enormous incongruity of all this triumphant satisfaction in the face of the inferiority which should be patent to all, seems only to be noticed by the few and the select. For all those who think with the public mind have blindfolded their eyes and closed their ears. The incongruity is not even acknowledged to exist. How is this possible? What power is sufficiently influential to deny this existence? What species of men must have attained to supremacy in Germany that feelings which are so strong and simple should be denied or prevented from obtaining expression? This power, this species of men, I will name – they are the *Philistines of Culture*.

As everyone knows, the word "Philistine" is borrowed from the vernacular of student-life, and, in its widest and most popular sense, it signifies the reverse of a son of the Muses, of an artist, and of the genuine man of culture. The Philistine of culture, however, the study of whose type and the hearing of whose confessions (when he makes them) have now become tiresome duties, distinguishes himself from the general notion of the order "Philistine" by means of a superstition: he fancies that he is himself a son of the Muses and a man of culture. This incomprehensible error clearly shows that he does not even know the difference between a Philistine and his opposite. We must not be surprised, therefore, if we find him, for the most part, solemnly protesting that he is no Philistine. Owing to this lack of self-knowledge, he is convinced that his "culture" is the consummate manifestation of real German culture; and, since he everywhere meets with scholars of his own type, since all public institutions, whether schools, universities, or academies, are so organized as to be in complete harmony with his education and needs, wherever he goes he bears with him the triumphant feeling that he is the worthy champion of prevailing German culture, and he frames his pretensions and claims accordingly. If, however, real culture takes unity of style for granted (and even an inferior and degenerate culture cannot be imagined in which a certain coalescence of the profusion of forms has not taken place), it is just possible that the confusion underlying the Culture-Philistine's error may arise from the fact that, since he comes into contact everywhere with creatures cast in the same mold as himself, he concludes that this uniformity among all "scholars" must point to a certain uniformity in German education – hence to culture.[(UM)]

Nobody, however, is more disliked by the Culture-Philistine than the man who regards him as a Philistine, and tells him what he is – namely, the barrier in the way of all powerful men and creators, the labyrinth for all who doubt and go astray, the swamp for all the weak and weary, the fetters of those who would run towards lofty goals, the poisonous mist that chokes all germinating hopes, the scorching sand to all those German thinkers who seek, and thirst after, a new life. For the mind of Germany is seeking; and ye hate it because it is seeking, and because it will not accept your word, when ye declare that ye have found what it is seeking. How could it have been possible for a type like that of the Culture-Philistine to develop? And even granting its development, how was it able to rise to the powerful Position of supreme judge concerning all questions of German culture? How could this have been possible, seeing that a whole procession of grand and heroic figures has already filed past us, whose every movement, the expression of whose every feature, whose questioning voice and burning eye betrayed the one fact, *that they were seekers*, and that they sought that which the Culture-Philistine had long fancied he had found – to wit, a genuine original German culture? Is there a soil – thus they seemed to ask – a soil that is pure enough, unhandselled enough, of sufficient virgin sanctity, to allow the mind of Germany to build its house upon it? Questioning thus, they wandered through the wilderness, and the woods of wretched ages and narrow conditions, and as seekers they disappeared from our vision; one of them, at an advanced age, was even able to stay, in the name of all: "For half a century my life has been hard and bitter enough; I have allowed myself no rest, but have ever striven, sought and done, to the best and to the utmost of my ability."

What does our Culture-Philistinism say of these seekers? It regards them simply as discoverers, and seems to forget that they themselves only claimed to be seekers. We have our culture, say her sons; for have we not our "classics?" Not only is the foundation there, but the building already stands upon it – we ourselves constitute that building. And, so saying, the Philistine raises his hand to his brow.

But, in order to be able thus to misjudge, and thus to grant left-handed veneration to our classics, people must have ceased to know them. This, generally speaking, is precisely what has happened. For, otherwise, one ought to know that there is only one way of honoring them, and that is to continue seeking with the same spirit and with the same courage, and not to weary of the search. But to foist the doubtful title of "classics" upon them, and to "edify" oneself from time to time by reading their works, means to yield to those feeble and selfish emotions which all the paying public may purchase at concert-halls and theatres. Even the raising of monuments to their memory, and the christening of feasts and societies with their names – all these things are but so many ringing cash payments by means of which the Culture-Philistine discharges his indebtedness to them, so that in all other respects he may be rid of them, and, above all, not bound to follow in their wake and prosecute his search further. For henceforth inquiry is to cease: that is the Philistine watchword.*(UM)*

– I spoke of German *esprit* to the effect that it becomes coarser and shallower. Is that enough? In reality, it is something quite different which frightens me; German seriousness, German profundity, and German *passion* in intellectual matters, are more and more on the decline. Pathos has altered, not merely intellectuality. – I come in contact now and then with German universities: what an atmosphere prevails among their scholars, what withered, contented, and lukewarm intellectuality! It would be a great misunderstanding if a person should adduce German science by way of objection to me, and, besides, it would be a proof that he had not read a word of my writings. For seventeen years I have not tired of showing the *intellectually enervating* influence of our modern scientific pursuits. The severe helotism to which the immense extent of the sciences at present condemns every individual, is a principal reason why the more fully, more richly and *more profoundly* endowed natures no longer find suitable education and suitable *educators*.*(T)*

"If you try to further the progress of science as quickly as possible, you will end by destroying it as quickly as possible; just as the hen is worn out which you force to lay too many eggs." The progress of science has been amazingly rapid in the last decade; but consider the savants, those exhausted hens. They are certainly not "harmonious" natures: they can merely cackle more than before, because they lay eggs oftener: but the eggs are always smaller, though their books are bigger. The natural result of it all is the favorite "popularizing" of science (or rather its feminizing and infantizing), the villainous habit of cutting the cloth of science to fit the figure of the "general public."[(UM)]

In my ideal state, I would cast out the so called "cultured," like Plato the poet: this is my terrorism. [(N)]

Consider the periods in a nation in which the learned man comes into prominence; they are the periods of exhaustion, often of sunset, of decay – the effervescing strength, the confidence in life, the confidence in the future are no more. The preponderance of the mandarins never signifies any good, any more than does the advent of democracy, or arbitration instead of war, equal rights for women, the religion of pity, and all the other symptoms of declining life.[(GM)]

When a foreigner wishes to familiarize himself with our universities, first he emphatically asks: "How do students relate to the university?" We answer: "With our ears, as listeners." The foreigner, surprised, asks once more, "Only with your ears?" "Only with our ears," we answer once again. The student listens. When he speaks, when he looks, when he socializes, when he drifts towards art, essentially, when he lives, he is autonomous, therefore independent from the educational institution. Most often the student writes while he listens. These are the moments in which he is attached to the university's umbilical cord. He can choose to hear what he wants to hear, he need not believe what he hears, and he can seal his ears shut when he desires not to listen. The professor, however, speaks to these listening students. Anything else he thinks and does is separated from his students' perception via a vast chasm. The professor frequently reads while he speaks. Generally speaking, he wants to have as many such listeners as possible, and in desperation he is content with a few, though almost never with one. A running mouth and many ears, with half as many writing hands – that is the external academic apparatus that functions within the university's education machine. The owner of this mouth is separate and independent from the owners of the many ears: this is the dual autonomy that is praised with elation as "academic freedom." Incidentally, to enhance this freedom further, he can say nearly all he wants, while the others can hear nearly all they want: yet at a slight distance behind both groups stands a certain, tense authority figure of the state, to remind them from time to time that *it* is the purpose, goal, and epitome of any outlandish speaking and listening procedures. *(N)*

Terrible danger: blending the mechanism of American politics with baseless academic culture.*(N)*

The haste quickens; thus education withers and becomes less every day. *(N)*

It is becoming ever more apparent that we lack the educational institutions we direly need. Our secondary schools, which were built to facilitate this sublime goal, have either become convalescent homes to a dubious culture that, with deep hatred, repels true aristocracy based on any kind of spirited education: or they produce an education that is micrological,[34] barren, or in any case completely void of actual learning, whose only worth has perhaps proven to at least dull the eyes and ears to the seduction of such a dubious culture. *(N)*

It would not yield success to hoist secondary schools onto the magnificent train of classical education, so says the foreign, un-German, cosmopolitan character of this educational endeavor with the belief that it is possible to move away from native soil beneath one's feet while at the same time standing firm in the delusion that one can leap hastily over bridges into the alienated Hellenic world through denial of the greater national German spirit. Admittedly, one must understand that to see this German spirit is to see where it lies hidden; under fashionable clothing, or beneath rubble – one must love it enough to not shame its withering form, and one must above all beware not to confuse

34 Micrological (Greek) = small, thoughtful.

himself with that which now pontificates proudly as "German culture of the present." With this, that spirit is far more inwardly hostile and currently within the sphere to despise the persistent lack of culture in the "present" that has often masked itself as the true German spirit, beneath rough surfaces beyond a perceivable form. What it now calls itself in contrast with especially dark "German culture" is a cosmopolitan power that acts like German spirit, like the journalist to Schiller, or like Meyerbeer to Beethoven: here works the strongest influence which, in the deepest fundamentals of the un-Germanic civilization of the French, talentlessly mimics and tastelessly imitates German society, press, art and style with a glossy veneer...

We cling firmly *to the* German spirit that revealed itself in the German Reformation, in German music, in the deep courage and severity of German philosophy, and in the recently tested loyalty of German soldiers, who fought and proved themselves in the face of an enemy's power, and therewith have we the right to expect a victory over the trendy pseudo culture of the "present." Involved in this fight are the true training schools, especially the secondary schools, and the adolescents of the new generation who are to ignite that which is truly German. This is our highest hope for the future fruit of the school: in which so-called classical education will finally reign once more in its natural place of origin.

A true renewal and purification of the secondary school will emerge only from a vast, ripe renewal and purification of the German spirit. Mysterious and elusive is the band which is tightly bound to the innermost German being and Greek genius. However, not before the noblest needs of the true German spirit are grasped by the hands of Greek genius akin to the firm grip of a barbarian torrent, not before this German spirit clamors at the Greeks with a starved yearning, not before the arduously gained insight into the Greek homeland which Schiller and Goethe exceeded, have all become shrines of the best and most talented men, will the goal of classical education in secondary school do anything other than flutter back and forth in the wind: at least they will not be blamed, those who desire to implant ever so limited science and scholarliness into secondary schools, yet have eyes on a firm, true and lasting ideal goal to save their schools from the allure of glistening phantoms who call themselves "culture" and "education." This is the most tragic situation of today's secondary schools: the most limited view points are regarded as correct because no one is capable of overthrowing, or at least even identifying, where these viewpoints are wrong.[(N)]

To merely gaze upon a young generation of Philologists; how rare it is to notice that shameful feeling that we have absolutely no right to exist in view of the Hellenic world, and how harshly the young brood builds their miserable nests against that feeling in the middle of the most magnificent temples! The vast majority of them, since their time at the university, so carelessly and shamelessly wander through the astonishing ruins of this world and cry out of every corner with a mighty voice: "away from here, you profane and uninitiated! Flee silently from this sanctuary, silent and ashamed!" Alas, their voice cries out in vain: for one must already be molded in a Greek cast in order to understand Greek curses and spell wording! With ease, they barbarically invade the world beneath these ruins, bring all their modern comforts and hobbies with them, and even settle down behind ancient pillars and tombs: whereby they rejoice once they discover within these ancient ruins something they have been unknowingly practicing within themselves. The first one creates verse and understands how to consult the lexicon of Hesychius:[35] therefore he is immediately convinced he is the destined poetic translator of Æschylus, and even finds believers who assert that he, the poetic thief, is the "kindred spirit" of Æschylus! A second looks at all discrepancies and their shadows with the suspicious eyes of a police officer seeking Homer's guilt: he wastes his life tearing apart and connecting Homeric fragments, out of which he creates his own heroic guise. A third is uncomfortable with all

35 Hesychius, Greek academic, supposedly in 5 B.C. composed a lexicon based on older vocabulary that became a valuable resource for the poetic language of Greece.

the mysterious and orgiastic pages of antiquity: he determines once and for all to value only enlightened Apollo and finds a serene, wise and yet a somewhat amoral Apollonian entity in the Athenians. He can breathe only after he brings a dark angle of antiquity from the height of his own enlightenment yet again, when he, for example, discovers a brave brother in enlightened politics through Pythagoras. A fourth plagues himself with the question of why Oedipus was condemned to such terrible a fate as killing his father and marrying his mother. The guilt lies in poetic justice! Immediately he knows it: Oedipus was actually a passionate fellow devoid of any Christian softness: once he endured an unseemly heat when Tiresias[36] named him the cursed monster of the whole country. Perhaps Sophocles wants to teach, "be meek! Lest you then must kill your father and marry your mother!" Others rank themselves throughout their entire lives among verses of Greek and Roman poets and delight in the proportions 7:13 = 14:26. Finally, the fifth is promised a well rounded answer to the question regarding Homer from the view point of prepositions, believing he is pulling truth from the wells with ἀνά and κατά.[37] All of them, with their various tendencies, scour and scavenge Greek soil with a relentless, uncoordinated clumsiness that would strike fear into the heart of any serious friend of antiquity: and so, I want every man, talented or not, who has allowed himself to rise toward a certain professional inclination towards antiquity to grasp the hand that leads him to the following wisdom of perorieren:[38] "Do you also know, young man, what kind of dangers threaten you on your path of tremendous academic knowledge? Have you heard, after Aristotle's untragic death his statue will crumble? Currently you are threatened by this death. You wonder why? Then know this: philologists have tried for ages to reconstruct the fallen, buried statue of Greek antiquity, and until now it was always with inadequate power, for it is a colossus upon which only the few can climb about like dwarves. Tremendous joint efforts

36 Tiresias, legendary Greek seer.

37 ἀνά and κατά, Greek prepositions.

38 Perorieren (Latin) = to speak preparedly and overbearingly.

along with every levelling force of modern culture are applied: repeatedly, rarely before any dust is brushed off, it collapses and crushes mankind beneath it. This needs to be further addressed: everything must, for one reason or another, perish, but no one grasps this while they carefully try not to shatter the statue itself into pieces! The philologists perish because of the Greeks – that is something to overcome – but philologists shatter antiquity itself into pieces! Think about this, reckless young man. Run away, lest you become an iconoclast!"[(N)]

III

The New Values

Fundamental Idea: the new values must first be created – this remains *lost* to us![N]

Life

Wherever I found a living thing, there found I Will to Power; and even in the will of the servant found I the will to be master.

That to the stronger the weaker shall serve – thereto persuadeth he his will who would be master over a still weaker one. That delight alone he is unwilling to forego.

And as the lesser surrendereth himself to the greater that he may have delight and power over the least of all, so doth even the greatest surrender himself, and staketh – life, for the sake of power.

It is the surrender of the greatest to run risk and danger, and play dice for death.

And where there is sacrifice and service and love-glances, there also is the will to be master. By by-ways doth the weaker then slink into the fortress, and into the heart of the mightier one – and there stealeth power.

And this secret spake Life herself unto me. "Behold," said she, "I am that *which must ever surpass itself.*" [Z]

Good and evil, and rich and poor, and high and low, and all names of values: weapons shall they be, and sounding signs, that life must again and again surpass itself!

Aloft will it build itself with columns and stairs – life itself into remote distances would it gaze, and out towards blissful beauties – *therefore* doth it require elevation! *(Z)*

Our life should be ascents from peak to peak, though without flying or falling... *(N)*

Let your love to life be love to your highest hope; and let your highest hope be the highest thought of life! *(Z)*

Heathens are all who say yea to life, to whom "God" is the word for the great yea to everything. *(A)*

Life is a well of delight, but to him in whom the ruined stomach speaketh, the father of affliction, all fountains are poisoned. *(Z)*

We are proud of being no longer obliged to be liars, slanderers, and detractors of Life... *(WP)*

Primary tendencies:
1. To plant love into life, into one's *own* life on *every* level!
2. To be the only *antagonist* against everyone and everything that seeks to denigrate the value of life. *(N)*

When the centre of gravity of life is placed, *not* in life, but in the "other world" – *in nothingness* – life has in reality been deprived of its centre of gravity. *(A)*

Let us place the image of eternity upon *our* life! This thought covers more than any religion which condemns life as ephemeral and teaches one to take a second glance toward an indefinite *other.* *(N)*

We do not look forward to transcendental, unknown bliss, *blessings*, and *forgiveness,* but rather live life like we want to live it over and over again, like we want to live eternally! Our task reflects upon us in every moment. *(N)*

To have and to want more, *growth,* with one word – that is life itself.[(N)]

"One is continually promoting the interests of one's '*ego*' at the cost of other people"; "Living consists in living at the cost of others" – he who has not grasped this fact, has not taken the first step towards truth to himself. [(WP)]

What is living? – Living – that is to continually eliminate from ourselves what is about to die; Living – that is to be cruel and inexorable towards all that becomes weak and old in ourselves, and not only in ourselves. [(GS)]

From the military school of life. – What does not kill me, strengthens me.[(T)]

Each individual may be looked at with respect to whether he represents an ascending or a descending line of life.[(T)]

The ill constituted, the weak, impoverish life: the lively, the strong, enrich life... The former is life's parasite: the latter a perpetually giving gift.[(N)]

Let your life be a hundred-fold trial, your failures and accomplishments proof, and concern yourself with whether anyone knows about what you have tried and accomplished.[(N)]

The love of life is the antithesis to the love of long life. All love focuses on the moment and eternity – but *never* on "the length."[(N)]

To live is ever to be in danger. [(UM)]

On the hourglass of life. Life is full of rare individual moments of the greatest significance and infinite intervals which, at their best, let the shadows of those moments dance around us. Love, spring, a beautiful melody, the mountains, the moon, the sea – only once, they profoundly speak to our hearts: if ever they do find words. For many people never experience these moments, and are themselves intervals and pauses in the symphony of real life.[(H)]

The Second Dance Song

1.

"Into thine eyes gazed I lately, O Life: gold saw I gleam in thy night-eyes, – my heart stood still with delight:

– A golden bark saw I gleam on darkened waters, a sinking, drinking, reblinking, golden swing-bark!

At my dance-frantic foot, dost thou cast a glance, a laughing, questioning, melting, thrown glance:

Twice only movedst thou thy rattle with thy little hands – then did my feet swing with dance-fury. –

My heels reared aloft, my toes they hearkened, – thee they would know: hath not the dancer his ear – in his toe!

Unto thee did I spring: then fledst thou back from my bound; and towards me waved thy fleeing, flying tresses round!

Away from thee did I spring, and from thy snaky tresses: then stoodst thou there half-turned, and in thine eye caresses.

With crooked glances – dost thou teach me crooked courses; on crooked courses learn my feet – crafty fancies!

I fear thee near, I love thee far; thy flight allureth me, thy seeking secureth me: – I suffer, but for thee, what would I not gladly bear!

For thee, whose coldness inflameth, whose hatred misleadeth, whose flight enchaineth, whose mockery – pleadeth:

– Who would not hate thee, thou great bindress, in-windress, temptress, seekress, findress! Who would not love thee, thou innocent, impatient, wind-swift, child-eyed sinner!

Whither pullest thou me now, thou paragon and tomboy? And now foolest thou me fleeing; thou sweet romp dost annoy!

I dance after thee, I follow even faint traces lonely. Where art thou? Give me thy hand! Or thy finger only!

Here are caves and thickets: we shall go astray! – Halt! Stand still! Seest thou not owls and bats in fluttering fray?

Thou bat! Thou owl! Thou wouldst play me foul? Where are we? From the dogs hast thou learned thus to bark and howl.

Thou gnashest on me sweetly with little white teeth; thine evil eyes shoot out upon me, thy curly little mane from underneath!

This is a dance over stock and stone: I am the hunter, – wilt thou be my hound, or my chamois anon?

Now beside me! And quickly, wickedly springing! Now up! And over! – Alas! I have fallen myself overswinging!

Oh, see me lying, thou arrogant one, and imploring grace! Gladly would I walk with thee – in some lovelier place!

– In the paths of love, through bushes variegated, quiet, trim! Or there along the lake, where gold-fishes dance and swim!

Thou art now a-weary? There above are sheep and sun-set stripes: is it not sweet to sleep – the shepherd pipes?

Thou art so very weary? I carry thee thither; let just thine arm sink! And art thou thirsty – I should have something; but thy mouth would not like it to drink!

– Oh, that cursed, nimble, supple serpent and lurking-witch! Where art thou gone? But in my face do I feel through thy hand, two spots and red blotches itch!

I am verily weary of it, ever thy sheepish shepherd to be. Thou witch, if I have hitherto sung unto thee, now shalt *thou* – cry unto me!

To the rhythm of my whip shalt thou dance and cry! I forget not my whip? – Not I!" –

2.

Then did Life answer me thus, and kept thereby her fine ears closed:

"O Zarathustra! Crack not so terribly with thy whip! Thou knowest surely that noise killeth thought, – and just now there came to me such delicate thoughts.

We are both of us genuine ne'er-do-wells and ne'er-do-ills. Beyond good and evil found we our island and our green meadow – we two alone! Therefore must we be friendly to each other!

And even should we not love each other from the bottom of our hearts, – must we then have a grudge against each other if we do not love each other perfectly?

And that I am friendly to thee, and often too friendly, that knowest thou: and the reason is that I am envious of thy Wisdom. Ah, this mad old fool, Wisdom!

If thy Wisdom should one day run away from thee, ah! then would also my love run away from thee quickly." –

Thereupon did Life look thoughtfully behind and around, and said softly: "O Zarathustra, thou art not faithful enough to me!

Thou lovest me not nearly so much as thou sayest; I know thou thinkest of soon leaving me.

There is an old heavy, heavy, booming-clock: it boometh by night up to thy cave –

– When thou hearest this clock strike the hours at midnight, then thinkest thou between one and twelve thereon –

– Thou thinkest thereon, O Zarathustra, I know it – of soon leaving me!" –

"Yea," answered I, hesitatingly, "but thou knowest it also" – And I said something into her ear, in amongst her confused, yellow, foolish tresses.

"Thou *knowest* that, O Zarathustra? That knoweth no one" –

And we gazed at each other, and looked at the green meadow o'er which the cool evening was just passing, and we wept together. –

Then, however, was Life dearer unto me than all my Wisdom had ever been. –

Thus spake Zarathustra.

3.

One!

O man! Take heed!

Two!

What saith deep midnight's voice indeed?

Three!

"I slept my sleep –

Four!

"From deepest dream I've woke and plead: –
Five!
"The world is deep,
Six!
"And deeper than the day could read.
Seven!
"Deep is its woe –
Eight!
"Joy – deeper still than grief can be:
Nine!
"Woe saith: Hence! Go!
Ten!
"But joys all want eternity –
Eleven!
"Want deep profound eternity!"
Twelve! (Z)

Man

Man is difficult to discover, and unto himself most difficult of all; often lieth the spirit concerning the soul. So causeth the spirit of gravity. [(Z)]

A thousand paths are there which have never yet been trodden; a thousand salubrities and hidden islands of life. Unexhausted and undiscovered is still man and man's world. [(Z)]

I have searched among people and have not found my ideal among them. [(N)]

Man is a rope stretched between the animal and the Superman – a rope over an abyss.

A dangerous crossing, a dangerous wayfaring, a dangerous looking-back, a dangerous trembling and halting.

What is great in man is that he is a bridge and not a goal: what is lovable in man is that he is an *over-going* and a *down-going*. [(Z)]

I love those that know not how to live except as down-goers, for they are the over-goers.

I love the great despisers, because they are the great adorers, and arrows of longing for the other shore.

I love those who do not first seek a reason beyond the stars for going down and being sacrifices, but sacrifice themselves to the earth, that the earth of the Superman may hereafter arrive.

I love him who liveth in order to know, and seeketh to know in order that the Superman may hereafter live. Thus seeketh he his own down-going.

I love him who laboreth and inventeth, that he may build the house for the Superman, and prepare for him earth, animal, and plant: for thus seeketh he his own down-going.

I love him who loveth his virtue: for virtue is the will to down-going, and an arrow of longing.

I love him who reserveth no share of spirit for himself, but wanteth to be wholly the spirit of his virtue: thus walketh he as spirit over the bridge.

I love him who maketh his virtue his inclination and destiny: thus, for the sake of his virtue, he is willing to live on, or live no more.

I love him who desireth not too many virtues. One virtue is more of a virtue than two, because it is more of a knot for one's destiny to cling to.

I love him whose soul is lavish, who wanteth no thanks and doth not give back: for he always bestoweth, and desireth not to keep for himself.

I love him who is ashamed when the dice fall in his favour, and who then asketh: "Am I a dishonest player?" – for he is willing to succumb.

I love him who scattereth golden words in advance of his deeds, and always doeth more than he promiseth: for he seeketh his own down-going.

I love him who justifieth the future ones, and redeemeth the past ones: for he is willing to succumb through the present ones.

I love him who chasteneth his God, because he loveth his God: for he must succumb through the wrath of his God.

I love him whose soul is deep even in the wounding, and may

succumb through a small matter: thus goeth he willingly over the bridge.

I love him whose soul is so overfull that he forgetteth himself, and all things are in him: thus all things become his down-going.

I love him who is of a free spirit and a free heart: thus is his head only the bowels of his heart; his heart, however, causeth his down-going.

I love all who are like heavy drops falling one by one out of the dark cloud that lowereth over man: they herald the coming of the lightning, and succumb as heralds.

Lo, I am a herald of the lightning, and a heavy drop out of the cloud: the lightning, however, is the *Superman*. – *(Z)*

The most careful ask today: "How is man to be maintained?"

Zarathustra however asketh, as the first and only one: "How is man to be *surpassed?*"

The Superman, I have at heart; *that* is the first and only thing to Me – and *not* man: not the neighbor, not the poorest, not the sorriest, not the best. –

O my brethren, what I can love in man is that he is an over-going and a down-going. *(Z)*

I teach you the Superman. Man is something that is to be surpassed. What have ye done to surpass man?

All beings hitherto have created something beyond themselves: and ye want to be the ebb of that great tide, and would rather go back to the beast than surpass man?

What is the ape to man? A laughing-stock, a thing of shame. And just the same shall man be to the Superman: a laughing-stock, a thing of shame.

Ye have made your way from the worm to man, and much within you is still worm. Once were ye apes, and even yet man is more of an ape than any of the apes.

Even the wisest among you is only a disharmony and hybrid of plant and phantom. But do I bid you become phantoms or plants?

Lo, I teach you the Superman! *The Superman* is the meaning of the earth. Let your will say: The Superman *shall be* the meaning of the earth! *(Z)*

The antithesis of the *Superman* is the *last* man: I created him in his own likeness. *(N)*

Lo! I show you *the last man.*

"What is love? What is creation? What is longing? What is a star?" – so asketh the last man and blinketh.

The earth hath then become small, and on it there hoppeth the last man who maketh everything small. His species is ineradicable like that of the ground-flea; the last man liveth longest.

"We have discovered happiness" – say the last men, and blink thereby.

They have left the regions where it is hard to live; for they need warmth. One still loveth one's neighbor and rubbeth against him; for one needeth warmth.

Turning ill and being distrustful, they consider sinful: they walk warily. He is a fool who still stumbleth over stones or men!

A little poison now and then: that maketh pleasant dreams. And much poison at last for a pleasant death.

One still worketh, for work is a pastime. But one is careful lest the pastime should hurt one.

One no longer becometh poor or rich; both are too burdensome. Who still wanteth to rule? Who still wanteth to obey? Both are too burdensome.

No shepherd, and one herd! Everyone wanteth the same; everyone is equal: he who hath other sentiments goeth voluntarily into the madhouse.

"Formerly all the world was insane," – say the subtlest of them, and blink thereby.

They are clever and know all that hath happened: so there is no end to their raillery. People still fall out, but are soon reconciled – otherwise it spoileth their stomachs.

They have their little pleasures for the day, and their little pleasures for the night, but they have a regard for health.

"We have discovered happiness," – say the last men, and blink thereby. –[(Z)]

None of you fight for justice, you, the righteous, but rather for the victory of your image of man. And with my image of the Superman I *shatter all of your images of man*: behold, this is *Zarathustra's will to justice.*[(N)]

The goal is not "humanity," but rather the *Superman*![(N)]

Humanity must aim its goal far above and outside itself – but not in a fake world, rather in its own *perpetuation.*[(N)]

Let man be a means to something that is no longer man. *(N)*

We want to immerse humanity within nature and thereby absolve it of its divine masquerade. We want to take what we need from nature in order to make dreams of men. Something that *is more sublime* than a storm, than mountains and the sea, must sprout forth as the son of man! *(N)*

One thing in this whole world that truly concerns us, grows in our needs, ambitions, joys, hopes, colors, directions, fantasies, devotions, and banes is that we have *created man*, and we have *forgotten* it. Thus have we conceived of yet another creator in retrospect for everything, or is the problem with us about *where from* we are annihilated through suffering? *(N)*

I want to reclaim the sublime beauty within the real and conceited things we gave away as the property and product of man, as his most beautiful Apologie.[39] Man as poet, thinker, God, love, power – oh, he poured over this mighty bounty as he surrendered it in order to *impoverish* and thrust himself into bale and woe! Until now that was the greatest selflessness he marveled at and worshipped, with which he knowingly created an admirable mask for himself. *(N)*

The majority of people are only piecemeal and fragmentary examples of man: only when all these creatures are jumbled together does one whole man arise. Whole ages and whole peoples in this sense, have a fragmentary character about them; it may perhaps be part of the economy of human development that man should develop himself only piecemeal. But, for this reason, one should not forget that the only important consideration is the rise of the synthetic man; that inferior men, and by far the great majority of people, are but rehearsals and exercises out of which here and there *a whole man* may arise; a man who is a human milestone, and who indicates how far mankind has advanced up to a certain point. *(WP)*

39 Apologie (Greek) = plea, defensiveness.

I teach thus: there are higher and lower people, and an individual can justify his existence for entire centuries within these circumstances – that is a full, rich, great and complete man in respect to infinite, fragmentary, shattered people.[(N)]

Mankind has no worthwhile goals other than great men and great works.[(N)]

How do men attain to great power and to great tasks? All the virtues and proficiencies of the body and the soul are little by little laboriously acquired, through great industry, self-control, and keepings one's self within narrow bounds, through a frequent, energetic, and genuine repetition of the same work and of the same hardships; but there are men who are the heirs and masters of this slowly acquired and manifold treasure of virtues and proficiencies – because, owing to happy and reasonable marriages and also to lucky accidents, the acquired and accumulated forces of many generations, instead of being squandered and subdivided, have been assembled together by means of steadfast struggling and willing. And thus, in the end, a man appears who is such a monster of strength, that he craves for a monstrous task.[(WP)]

Man's Values

The Body

I conjure you, my brethren, *remain true to the earth*, and believe not those who speak unto you of superearthly hopes! Poisoners are they, whether they know it or not.

Despisers of life are they, decaying ones and poisoned ones themselves, of whom the earth is weary: so away with them!

Once blasphemy against God was the greatest blasphemy; but God died, and therewith also those blasphemers. To blaspheme the earth is now the dreadfulest sin, and to rate the heart of the unknowable higher than the meaning of the earth! [(Z)]

A new pride taught me mine ego, and that teach I unto men: no longer to thrust one's head into the sand of celestial things, but to carry it freely, a terrestrial head, which giveth meaning to the earth!

A new will teach I unto men: to choose that path which man hath followed blindly, and to approve of it – and no longer to slink aside from it, like the sick and perishing!

The sick and perishing – it was they who despised the body and the earth, and invented the heavenly world, and the redeeming blood-drops; but even those sweet and sad poisons they borrowed from the body and the earth!

From their misery they sought escape, and the stars were too remote for them. Then they sighed: "O that there were heavenly paths by which to steal into another existence and into happiness!" Then they contrived for themselves their by-paths and bloody draughts!

Beyond the sphere of their body and this earth they now fancied themselves transported, these ungrateful ones. But to what did they owe the convulsion and rapture of their transport? To their body and this earth.

Gentle is Zarathustra to the sickly. Verily, he is not indignant at their modes of consolation and ingratitude. May they become convalescents and overcomers, and create higher bodies for themselves! *(Z)*

The Despisers of the Body

To the despisers of the body will I speak my word. I wish them neither to learn afresh, nor teach anew, but only to bid farewell to their own bodies, – and thus be dumb.

"Body am I, and soul" – so saith the child. And why should one not speak like children?

But the awakened one, the knowing one, saith: "Body am I entirely, and nothing more; and soul is only the name of something in the body."

The body is a big sagacity, a plurality with one sense, a war and a peace, a flock and a shepherd.

An instrument of thy body is also thy little sagacity, my brother, which thou callest "spirit" – a little instrument and plaything of thy big sagacity.

"Ego," sayest thou, and art proud of that word. But the greater thing – in which thou art unwilling to believe – is thy body with its big sagacity; it saith not "ego," but doeth it.

What the sense feeleth, what the spirit discerneth, hath never its end in itself. But sense and spirit would fain persuade thee that they are the end of all things: so vain are they.

Instruments and playthings are sense and spirit: behind them there is still the Self. The Self seeketh with the eyes of the senses, it hearkeneth also with the ears of the spirit.

Ever hearkeneth the Self, and seeketh; it compareth, mastereth, conquereth, and destroyeth. It ruleth, and is also the ego's ruler.

Behind thy thoughts and feelings, my brother, there is a mighty lord, an unknown sage – it is called Self; it dwelleth in thy body, it is thy body.

There is more sagacity in thy body than in thy best wisdom. And who then knoweth why thy body requireth just thy best wisdom?

Thy Self laugheth at thine ego, and its proud prancings. "What are these prancings and flights of thought unto me?" it saith to itself.

"A by-way to my purpose. I am the leading-string of the ego, and the prompter of its notions."

The Self saith unto the ego: "Feel pain!" And thereupon it suffereth, and thinketh how it may put an end thereto – and for that very purpose it is *meant* to think.

The Self saith unto the ego: "Feel pleasure!" Thereupon it rejoiceth, and thinketh how it may ofttimes rejoice – and for that very purpose it is *meant* to think.

To the despisers of the body will I speak a word. That they despise is caused by their esteem. What is it that created esteeming and despising and worth and will?

The creating Self created for itself esteeming and despising, it created for itself joy and woe. The creating body created for itself spirit, as a hand to its will.

Even in your folly and despising ye each serve your Self, ye despisers of the body. I tell you, your very Self wanteth to die, and turneth away from life.

No longer can your Self do that which it desireth most: – create beyond itself. That is what it desireth most; that is all its fervour.

But it is now too late to do so: – so your Self wisheth to succumb, ye despisers of the body.

To succumb – so wisheth your Self; and therefore have ye become despisers of the body. For ye can no longer create beyond yourselves.

And therefore are ye now angry with life and with the earth. And unconscious envy is in the sidelong look of your contempt.

I go not your way, ye despisers of the body! Ye are no bridges for me to the Superman! – Thus spake Zarathustra. [(Z)]

Remain true to the earth, my brethren, with the power of your virtue! Let your bestowing love and your knowledge be devoted to be the meaning of the earth! Thus do I pray and conjure you.

Let it not fly away from the earthly and beat against eternal walls with its wings! Ah, there hath always been so much flown-away virtue!

Lead, like me, the flown-away virtue back to the earth – yea, back to body and life: that it may give to the earth its meaning, a human meaning! [(Z)]

Let your spirit and your virtue be devoted to the sense of the earth, my brethren: let the value of everything be determined anew by you! Therefore shall ye be fighters! Therefore shall ye be creators! [(Z)]

Goal: greater cultivation of the entire *body*, not only the brain! (N)

The essential thing is to start out from the body and to use it as the general clue. It is by far the richer phenomenon, and allows of much more accurate observation. The belief in the body is much more soundly established than the belief in the spirit.(WP)

Spirit is life which itself cutteth into life: by its own torture doth it increase its own knowledge, – did you know that before? (Z)

Nothing is more dangerous than the self-sufficient "introspection" of the spirit... (N)

Not the *spirit*, but *spirituality* is the danger. (N)

"Spirit" is only a means and an instrument in the service of higher life, in the service of the elevation of life.(WP)

Formerly one saw in man's consciousness, in "spirit," the proof of his higher origin, of his Divinity; in order to *perfect* man, one advised him, after the manner of the tortoise to withdraw the senses into himself, to cease having intercourse with the earthly, to shuffle off the mortal coil: then the main part of him remained behind, "pure spirit." We have also given better thought to this matter: the fact of becoming conscious, "spirit," is regarded by us just as a symptom of the relative incompleteness of the organism, as an attempting, groping, mistaking, as a trouble by which unnecessarily much nerve-force is used up, – we deny that anything whatsoever can be made perfect as long as it is still made conscious. "Pure spirit" is a pure stupidity; when we deduct the nervous system and the senses, the "mortal coil," *our calculation is wrong* – that is all! (A)

A man can create a reasonably ideal body for himself – many systems work in the same manner, how many will work for and against one other, how much finesse will be placed on equilibrium and so forth, will be judged – all consciousness standing against this is narrow and indignant: that no soul is remotely sufficient to receive only that which can be provided by spirit, and perhaps the wisest professors and legislators must feel clumsy and amateurish amid the grinding gears of war, duty and justice. How little we will know! How often these few lead us to fallacies and blunders! Consciousness is just a *tool*: and considering that, how great and how high achievements will be without consciousness – though not the most necessary, but indeed the most admirable – on the contrary: perhaps there is a not so badly developed body, one that functions without a multitude of problems: it is just the last remaining body, thus a child – we forgive him his *childishness*! … Thus, we must reverse the hierarchy: everything "conscious" is only the *second most important*; it is *close* and *intimate* to us, and there is no reason, at least no moral reason, to deem it otherwise. The fact that we see what is *closest* to us as the *most relevant* is merely an old prejudice. Therefore, relearn it, with the underlying assessment! The spiritual is the innate sign language of the *body*! [(N)]

Good & Evil

What is good? – All that increases the feeling of power, the will to power, power itself, in man.

What is bad? – All that proceeds from weakness.

What is happiness? – The feeling that power *increases*, – that a resistance is overcome.

Not contentedness, but more power; *not* peace at any price, but warfare; *not* virtue but capacity (virtue in the Renaissance style, *virtù*, virtue free from any moralic acid). The weak and ill-constituted shall perish: first principle of *our* charity. And people shall help them to do so. What is more injurious than any crime? – Practical sympathy for all the ill-constituted and weak: – Christianity... *(A)*

The knightly-aristocratic "values" are based on a careful cult of the physical, on a flowering, rich, and even effervescing healthiness, that goes considerably beyond what is necessary for maintaining life, on war, adventure, the chase, the dance, the tourney – on everything, in fact, which is contained in strong, free, and joyous action. *(GM)*

Formerly it was said of every form of morality, "Ye shall know them by their fruits." I say of every form of morality: "It is a fruit, and from it I learn the *Soil* out of which it grew." *(WP)*

In a tour through the many finer and coarser moralities which have hitherto prevailed or still prevail on the earth, I found certain traits recurring regularly together, and connected with one another, until finally two primary types revealed themselves to me, and a radical distinction was brought to light. There is a *master-morality* and *slave-morality;* – I would at once add, however, that in all higher and mixed civilizations, there are also attempts at the reconciliation of the two moralities; but one finds still oftener the confusion and mutual misunderstanding of them, indeed, sometimes their close juxtaposition – even in the same man, within one soul. The distinctions of moral values have either originated in a ruling caste, pleasantly conscious of being different from the ruled – or among the ruled class, the slaves and dependents of all sorts. In the first case, when it is the rulers who determine the conception "good," it is the exalted, proud disposition which is regarded as the distinguishing feature, and that which determines the order of rank. The noble type of man separates from himself the beings in whom the opposite of this exalted, proud disposition displays itself: he despises them. Let it at once be noted that in this first kind of morality the antithesis "good" and "bad" means practically the same as "noble" and "despicable"; – the antithesis "good" and *"evil"* is of a different origin. The cowardly, the timid, the insignificant, and those thinking merely of narrow utility are despised; moreover, also, the distrustful, with their constrained glances, the self-abasing, the dog-like kind of men who let themselves be abused, the mendicant flatterers, and above all the liars: – it is a fundamental belief of all aristocrats that the common people are untruthful. "We truthful ones" – the nobility in ancient Greece called themselves. ... The noble type of man regards *himself* as a determiner of values; he does not require to be approved of; he passes the judgment: "What is injurious to me is injurious in itself"; he knows that it is he himself only who confers honor on things; he is a *creator of values.* He honors whatever he recognizes in himself: such morality is self-glorification. In the foreground there is the feeling of plentitude, of power, which seeks to overflow, the happiness of high tension, the consciousness of a wealth which would fain give and bestow: – the noble man also helps the unfortunate, but not – or scarcely – out of pity, but rather from an impulse generated by the super-abundance of power. The noble man honors in himself the powerful one, him also who has power over himself, who knows how to speak and how to keep silence, who takes pleasure in subjecting himself to severity and hardness, and has reverence for all that is severe and hard. "Wotan placed a hard heart in my breast," says an old Scandinavian Saga: it is thus rightly expressed from the soul of a proud Viking. Such a type of man is even proud of *not* being made for sympathy; the hero of the Saga therefore adds warningly: "He who has not a hard heart when young, will never have one." … – It is otherwise with the second type of morality, *slave-morality.* Supposing that the abused, the oppressed, the suffering, the unemancipated, the weary, and those uncertain of themselves, should moralize, what will be the common element in their moral estimates? Probably a pessimistic suspicion with regard to the entire situation of man will find expression, perhaps a condemnation of man, together with his situation. The slave has an unfavorable eye for the virtues of the powerful; he has a skepticism and distrust, a *refinement* of distrust of everything "good" that is there honored – he would fain persuade himself that the very happiness there is not genuine. On the other hand, *those* qualities which serve to alleviate the existence of sufferers are brought into prominence and flooded with light; it is here these are the most useful qualities, and almost the only means of supporting the burden of existence. Slave-morality is essentially the morality of utility. Here is the seat of the origin of the famous antitheses "good" and "evil": – power and dangerousness are assumed to reside in the evil, a certain dreadfulness, subtlety, and strength, which do not admit of being despised. According to slave-morality, therefore, the "evil" man arouses fear; according to master-morality, it is precisely the "good" man who arouses fear and seeks to arouse it, while the bad man is regarded as the despicable being.*(GE)*

There is an old illusion – it is called good and evil. Around soothsayers and astrologers hath hitherto revolved the orbit of this illusion.

Once did one *believe* in soothsayers and astrologers; and *therefore* did one believe, "Everything is fate: thou shalt, for thou must!"

Then again did one distrust all soothsayers and astrologers; and *therefore* did one believe, "Everything is freedom: thou canst, for thou willest!"

O my brethren, concerning the stars and the future there hath hitherto been only illusion, and not knowledge; and *therefore* concerning good and evil there hath hitherto been only illusion and not knowledge! [Z]

When I came unto men, then found I them resting on an old infatuation: all of them thought they had long known what was good and bad for men.

An old wearisome business seemed to them all discourse about virtue; and he who wished to sleep well spake of "good" and "bad" ere retiring to rest.

This somnolence did I disturb when I taught that *no one yet knoweth* what is good and bad: – unless it be the creating one!

– It is he, however, who createth man's goal, and giveth to the earth its meaning and its future: he only *effecteth* it *that* aught is good or bad.

And I bade them upset their old academic chairs, and wherever that old infatuation had sat; I bade them laugh at their great moralists, their saints, their poets, and their Saviours.

At their gloomy sages did I bid them laugh, and whoever had sat admonishing as a black scarecrow on the tree of life.

On their great grave-highway did I seat myself, and even beside the carrion and vultures – and I laughed at all their bygone and its mellow decaying glory. [Z]

The world is neither good nor evil! And so is it with man! [N]

Verily, I say unto you: good and evil which would be everlasting

– it doth not exist! Of its own accord must it ever surpass itself anew.

With your values and formulae of good and evil, ye exercise power, ye valuing ones: and that is your secret love, and the sparkling, trembling, and overflowing of your souls.

But a stronger power groweth out of your values, and a new surpassing: by it breaketh egg and egg-shell.

And he who hath to be a creator in good and evil – verily, he hath first to be a destroyer, and break values in pieces. *(Z)*

Life is spoiled by good and evil, which have exhausted your will, along with your values themselves, which long for death. *(N)*

You will always have morals, and only those that match your power. *(N)*

Every prevailing morality to any extent always strove toward the breed and cultivation of a specific type of man on the condition that it arrived solely at this type: thus, always under the condition of a certain type. Every morality believes that *with intent* and force many can be changed, and "made better" – they always view the assimilation of the standard type as "improvement" (they grasp no other concept). *(N)*

It requires minimal reflection in order to accept the idea that nothing is "good in itself," that something good must be thought of only as "wherefore good," by necessity, any good intentions will be viewed as "evil and bad" by opposing intentions: in short, every single thing to which we attribute the title "good," can also be denoted as "evil." *(N)*

Ye flee from me? Ye are frightened? Ye tremble at this word?

O my brethren, when I enjoined you to break up the good, and the tables of the good, then only did I embark man on his high seas.

And now only cometh unto him the great terror, the great outlook, the great sickness, the great nausea, the great sea-sickness.

False shores and false securities did the good teach you; in the lies of the good were ye born and bred. Everything hath been radically contorted and distorted by the good.

But he who discovered the country of "man," discovered also the country of "man's future." Now shall ye be sailors for me, brave, patient!

Keep yourselves up betimes, my brethren, learn to keep yourselves up! The sea stormeth: many seek to raise themselves again by you.

The sea stormeth: all is in the sea. Well! Cheer up! Ye old seaman-hearts!

What of fatherland! *Thither* striveth our helm where our *children's land* is! Thitherwards, stormier than the sea, stormeth our great longing! – [(Z)]

Man & Woman

Old and Young Women

"Why stealest thou along so furtively in the twilight, Zarathustra? And what hidest thou so carefully under thy mantle?

Is it a treasure that hath been given thee? Or a child that hath been born thee? Or goest thou thyself on a thief's errand, thou friend of the evil?" –

Verily, my brother, said Zarathustra, it is a treasure that hath been given me: it is a little truth which I carry.

But it is naughty, like a young child; and if I hold not its mouth, it screameth too loudly.

As I went on my way alone today, at the hour when the sun declineth, there met me an old woman, and she spake thus unto my soul:

"Much hath Zarathustra spoken also to us women, but never spake he unto us concerning woman."

And I answered her: "Concerning woman, one should only talk unto men."

"Talk also unto me of woman," said she; "I am old enough to forget it presently."

And I obliged the old woman and spake thus unto her:

Everything in woman is a riddle, and everything in woman hath one Solution – it is called pregnancy.

Man is for woman a means: the purpose is always the child. But what is woman for man?

Two different things wanteth the true man: danger and diversion. Therefore wanteth he woman, as the most dangerous plaything.

Man shall be trained for war, and woman for the recreation of the warrior: all else is folly.

Too sweet fruits – these the warrior liketh not. Therefore liketh he woman; – bitter is even the sweetest woman.

Better than man doth woman understand children, but man is more childish than woman.

In the true man there is a child hidden: it wanteth to play. Up then, ye women, and discover the child in man!

A plaything let woman be, pure and fine like the precious stone, illumined with the virtues of a world not yet come.

Let the beam of a star shine in your love! Let your hope say: "May I bear the Superman!"

In your love let there be valour! With your love shall ye assail him who inspireth you with fear!

In your love be your honor! Little doth woman understand otherwise about honor. But let this be your honor: always to love more than ye are loved, and never be the second.

Let man fear woman when she loveth: then maketh she every sacrifice, and everything else she regardeth as worthless.

Let man fear woman when she hateth: for man in his innermost soul is merely evil; woman, however, is mean.

Whom hateth woman most? – Thus spake the iron to the loadstone: "I hate thee most, because thou attractest, but art too weak to draw unto thee."

The happiness of man is, “I will.” The happiness of woman is, “He will.”

“Lo! now hath the world become perfect!” – thus thinketh every woman when she obeyeth with all her love.

Obey, must the woman, and find a depth for her surface. Surface is Woman’s soul, a mobile, stormy film on shallow water.

Man’s soul, however, is deep, its current gusheth in subterranean caverns: woman surmiseth its force, but comprehendeth it not. –

Then answered me the old woman: “Many fine things hath Zarathustra said, especially for those who are young enough for them.

Strange! Zarathustra knoweth little about woman, and yet he is right about them! Doth this happen, because with women nothing is impossible?

And now accept a little truth by way of thanks! I am old enough for it!

Swaddle it up and hold its mouth: otherwise it will scream too loudly, the little truth.”

“Give me, woman, thy little truth!” said I. And thus spake the old woman:

“Thou goest to women? Do not forget thy whip!” –Thus spake Zarathustra. *(Z)*

Man’s attribute is will, woman’s attribute is willingness, – such is the law of the sexes... *(GS)*

Thus would I have man and woman: fit for war, the one; fit for maternity, the other; both, however, fit for dancing with head and legs. *(Z)*

A woman needs children, man is always only a means, thus spake Zarathustra. "The emancipation of women," – this is the instinctive hatred of physiologically botched – that is to say, barren – women for those of their sisters who are well constituted: the fight against "man" is always only a means, a pretext, a piece of strategy. *(EH)*

"When women want to go to children, do not let her get accustomed to going to the child, but rather to men!" Says an old midwife. *(N)*

In no way are we foolish chastity-peddlers: when man needs a woman, he finds a woman, without the need to create or destroy a marriage.*(N)*

Preaching of chastity is a public incitement to unnatural practices. All depreciation of the sexual life, all the sullying of it by means of the concept "impure," is the essential crime against Life – is the essential crime against the Holy Spirit of Life. *(EH)*

Child & Marriage

I have a question for thee alone, my brother: like a sounding-lead, cast I this question into thy soul, that I may know its depth.

Thou art young, and desirest child and marriage. But I ask thee: Art thou a man *entitled* to desire a child?

Art thou the victorious one, the self-conqueror, the ruler of thy passions, the master of thy virtues? Thus do I ask thee.

Or doth the animal speak in thy wish, and necessity? Or isolation? Or discord in thee?

I would have thy victory and freedom long for a child. Living monuments shalt thou build to thy victory and emancipation.

Beyond thyself shalt thou build. But first of all must thou be built thyself, rectangular in body and soul.

Not only onward shalt thou propagate thyself, but upward! For that purpose may the garden of marriage help thee!

A higher body shalt thou create, a first movement, a spontaneously rolling wheel – a creating one shalt thou create.

Marriage: so call I the will of the twain to create the one that is more than those who created it. The reverence for one another, as those exercising such a will, call I marriage.

Let this be the significance and the truth of thy marriage. But that which the many-too-many call marriage, those superfluous ones – ah, what shall I call it?

Ah, the poverty of soul in the twain! Ah, the filth of soul in the twain! Ah, the pitiable self-complacency in the twain!

Marriage they call it all; and they say their marriages are made in heaven.

Well, I do not like it, that heaven of the superfluous! No, I do not like them, those animals tangled in the heavenly toils!

Far from me also be the God who limpeth thither to bless what he hath not matched!

Laugh not at such marriages! What child hath not had reason to weep over its parents?

Worthy did this man seem, and ripe for the meaning of the earth: but when I saw his wife, the earth seemed to me a home for madcaps.

Yea, I would that the earth shook with convulsions when a saint and a goose mate with one another.

This one went forth in quest of truth as a hero, and at last got for himself a small decked-up lie: his marriage he calleth it.

That one was reserved in intercourse and chose choicely. But one time he spoilt his company for all time: his marriage he calleth it.

Another sought a handmaid with the virtues of an angel. But all at once he became the handmaid of a woman, and now would he need also to become an angel.

Careful, have I found all buyers, and all of them have astute eyes. But even the astutest of them buyeth his wife in a sack.

Many short follies – that is called love by you. And your marriage putteth an end to many short follies, with one long stupidity.

Your love to woman, and woman's love to man – ah, would that it were sympathy for suffering and veiled deities! But generally two animals alight on one another.

But even your best love is only an enraptured simile and a painful ardour. It is a torch to light you to loftier paths.

Beyond yourselves shall ye love some day! Then *learn* first of all to love. And on that account ye had to drink the bitter cup of your love.

Bitterness is in the cup even of the best love; thus doth it cause longing for the Superman; thus doth it cause thirst in thee, the creating one!

Thirst in the creating one, arrow and longing for the Superman: tell me, my brother, is this thy will to marriage?

Holy call I such a will, and such a marriage. – Thus spake Zarathustra. [(Z)]

Your marriage-arranging: see that it be not a bad *arranging*! Ye have arranged too hastily: so there followeth therefrom – marriage-breaking!

And better marriage-breaking than marriage-bending, marriage-lying! – Thus spake a woman unto me: "Indeed, I broke the marriage, but first did the marriage break – me!" [(Z)]

I despise your law of marriage: I am disgusted by its fat fingers that demonstrate the right of the man. What I desire is to hear you speak of and believe the right *to* marry, a rare right: but *in* marriage there is only responsibility and no rights.[(N)]

Concerning the future of marriage. A supertax on inherited property, a longer term of military service for bachelors of a certain minimum age within the community.

Privileges of all sorts for fathers who lavish boys upon the world, and perhaps plural votes as well.

A medical certificate as a condition of any marriage, endorsed by the parochial authorities, in which a series of questions addressed to the parties and the medical officers must be answered ("family histories").

As a counter-agent to prostitution, or as its ennoblement, I would recommend leasehold marriages (to last for a term of years or months), with adequate provision for the children. Every marriage to be warranted and sanctioned by a certain number of good men and true, of the parish, as a parochial obligation.[(WP)]

The prerequisite for procreation should be the will, a reflection and a *desire* of the parents to pass on their love, as a monument of their unity: indeed, an *accomplishment of the drive toward unity* through a new being.[(N)]

Propagation as the holiest cause – pregnancy, the creation of the man and woman, the child, in which they will love seeing and *endowing a monument to* their *unity*.[(N)]

To have a descendant – above all, makes men steady, coherent, and able to provide: it is the best discipline.[(N)]

The privilege of fathering children should be granted as an honor, and will be seen in every light as a means of channeling natural carnal desires toward proactive propagation: otherwise the *lowly disposed* men will gain the upper hand, as higher spirits are not keen on merely erotic ventures. They are, without a doubt, the brave and warlike, and they owe this entirely to the best type of men who still exist. However, commercialism vies for superiority over the warlike, so...[(N)]

Exceptional individual men should have the chance to procreate with more than one woman; and individual women, especially those with favorable qualities, should likewise not remain bound to the fate of *one* man.*(N)*

Let us be against the ill gotten as we are against criminals: also, let us *detest* their propagation. This is the first general improvement of custom I desire: it should not be acceptable for the criminals and the ill gotten to propagate.*(N)*

Another commandment of philanthropy. There are cases where to have a child would be a crime – for example, for chronic invalids and extreme neurasthenics. ... Lastly, society here has a positive duty to fulfill, and of all the demands that are made on it, there are few more urgent and necessary than this one. Society, as the trustee of life, is responsible for every botched life before it comes into existence, and as it has to atone for such lives, it ought consequently to make it impossible for them ever to see the light of day: it should in many cases actually prevent the act of procreation, and may, without any regard for rank, descent, or intellect, hold in readiness the most rigorous forms of compulsion and restriction, and, under certain circumstances, have recourse to castration. The Mosaic law, "Thou shalt do no murder," is a piece of ingenuous puerility compared with the earnestness of this forbidding of life to decadents, "Thou shalt not beget!!!" ... For life itself recognizes no solidarity or equality of rights between the healthy and unhealthy parts of an organism. The latter must at all cost be *eliminated*, lest the whole fall to pieces. *(WP)*

Reproduction

The new problem: whether or not *a few people* can rise to become a better race at the cost of others. Reproduction... [(N)]

A certain question constantly recurs to us; it is perhaps a seductive and evil question; may it be whispered into the ears of those who have a right to such doubtful problems – those strong souls of today whose dominion over themselves is unswerving: it is not high time, now that the type "gregarious animal" is developing ever more and more in Europe, to set about rearing, thoroughly, artificially, and consciously, an opposite type, and to attempt to establish the latter's virtues? And would not the democratic movement itself find for the first time a sort of goal, salvation, and justification, if some one appeared who availed himself of it – so that at last, beside its new and sublime product, slavery (for this must be the end of European democracy), that higher species of ruling and Caesarian spirits might also be produced, which would stand upon it, hold to it, and would elevate themselves through it? This new race would climb aloft to new and hitherto impossible things, to a broader vision, and to its task on earth.[(WP)]

What I desire to forthrightly seal with all my power:

a) there is no worse mistake than when one confuses *upbringing* with *domestication*: as it has already been done... Upbringing is, as I understand it, a means of cultivating tremendous power in mankind, so that the sexes may build upon the work of their ancestors – not only outward, but inward, as their own inner *might* organically outgrows them...

b) there is an extraordinary danger when one believes that mankind attains its *greatest* growth and strength when individuals become average, mediocre, and flabby... Mankind is an abstraction: the goal of *upbringing*, even in individual cases, shall only ever be to raise the *strongest* (the domesticated is weak, squandered waste).[(N)]

My philosophy reveals the triumphant thought through which all other systems of thought must ultimately perish. It is the great disciplinary thought: those races that cannot bear it are doomed; those which regard it as the greatest blessing are destined to rule. *(WP)*

The strong of the future. To what extent necessity on the one hand and accident on the other have attained to conditions from which a *stronger species* may be reared: this we are now able to understand and to bring about consciously; we can now create those conditions under which such an elevation is possible.*(WP)*

Discipline

To stand high enough, to rise to your own peak, you *must* discipline yourself![(N)]

If you truly desire *your* ideal, you must turn the tide against the entire world. [(N)]

I cannot see how anyone can make up for having missed going to a *good school* at the proper time. Such a person does not know himself; he walks through life without ever having learned to walk. His soft muscles betray themselves at every step. Occasionally life itself is merciful enough to make a man recover this lost and severe schooling: by means of periods of sickness, perhaps, which exact the utmost will-power and self-control; or by means of a sudden state of poverty, which threatens his wife and child, and which may force a man to such activity as will restore energy to his slackened tendons, and a *tough spirit* to his will to life. The most desirable thing of all, however, is, under all circumstances to have severe discipline *at the right time*, i.e., at that age when it makes us proud that people should expect great things from us. For this is what distinguishes hard schooling, as good schooling, from every other schooling, namely, that a good deal is demanded, that a good deal is severely exacted; that goodness, nay even excellence itself, is required as if it were normal; that praise is scanty, that leniency is nonexistent; that blame is sharp, practical, and without reprieve, and has no regard to talent and antecedents. We are in every way in need of such a school: and this holds good of corporeal as well as of spiritual things; it would be fatal to draw distinctions here! The same discipline makes the soldier and the scholar efficient; and, looked at more closely, there is no true scholar who has not the instincts of a true soldier in his veins. To be able to command and to be able to obey in a proud fashion; to keep one's place in rank and file, and yet to be ready at any moment to lead; to prefer danger to comfort; not to weigh what is permitted and what is forbidden in a tradesman's balance; to be more hostile to pettiness, slyness, and parasitism than to wickedness. What is it that one *learns* in a hard school? *To obey* and *to command.*[(WP)]

All education begins in direct opposition to today's so-called academic freedom – via obedience, subordination, chastity and servitude.[(N)]

One day, there will be no thought directed toward anything other than *discipline*.[(N)]

To raise great men is the highest, most noble task of mankind.[(N)]

Greatness

The task is to bring to light what we direly *love and adore*, also what cannot be robbed through any subsequent gnosis: the great man. [(N)]

Every great man has a power which operates backward; all history is again placed on the scales on his account, and a thousand secrets of the past crawl out of their lurking-places – into *his* sunlight. There is absolutely no knowing what history may be some day. The past is still perhaps undiscovered in its essence! There is yet so much reinterpreting ability needed![(GS)]

Great men, like great periods, are explosive materials in which an immense force is accumulated; it is always prerequisite for such men, historically and physiologically, that for a long period there has been a collecting, a heaping up, an economizing, and a hoarding, with respect to them, – that for a long time no explosion has taken place.[(T)]

The great man must order and *establish*, *apply* and *demand* his own appreciation. [(N)]

Knowest thou not who is most needed by all? He who commandeth great things.

To execute great things is difficult: but the more difficult task is to command great things. [(Z)]

Greatness means to give direction. No river is great and abundant in and of itself: it is because it absorbs and carries forth the many streams that make it so. Likewise, it is so with all greatness of the spirit. It only depends upon one illuminating the direction which the many inflowing streams then must follow, not upon whether one is poorly or richly gifted from the beginning.[(H)]

My formula for greatness in man is *amor fati:*[40] the fact that a man wishes nothing to be different, either in front of him or behind him, or for all eternity. Not only must the necessary be borne, and on no account concealed, – all idealism is falsehood in the face of necessity, – but it must also be *loved...* *(EH)*

What Belongs to Greatness. – Who can attain to anything great if he does not feel himself the force and will *to inflict* great pain? The ability to suffer is a small matter: in that line, weak women and even slaves often attain masterliness. But not to perish from internal distress and doubt when one inflicts great suffering and hears the cry of it – that is great, that belongs to greatness. *(GS)*

The Wanderer

Then, when it was about midnight, Zarathustra went his way over the ridge of the isle, that he might arrive early in the morning at the other coast; because there he meant to embark. For there was a good roadstead there, in which foreign ships also liked to anchor: those ships took many people with them, who wished to cross over from the Happy Isles. So when Zarathustra thus ascended the mountain, he thought on the way of his many solitary wanderings from youth onwards, and how many mountains and ridges and summits he had already climbed.

I am a wanderer and mountain-climber, said he to his heart. I love not the plains, and it seemeth I cannot long sit still.

And whatever may still overtake me as fate and experience – a wandering will be therein, and a mountain-climbing: in the end one experienceth only oneself.

The time is now past when accidents could befall me; and what *could* now fall to my lot which would not already be mine own!

It returneth only, it cometh home to me at last – mine own Self,

40 Amor Fati (Latin) = Love of one's fate.

and such of it as hath been long abroad, and scattered among things and accidents.

And one thing more do I know: I stand now before my last summit, and before that which hath been longest reserved for me. Ah, my hardest path must I ascend! Ah, I have begun my lonesomest wandering!

He, however, who is of my nature doth not avoid such an hour: the hour that saith unto him: Now only dost thou go the way to thy greatness! Summit and abyss – these are now comprised together!

Thou goest the way to thy greatness: now hath it become thy last refuge, what was hitherto thy last danger!

Thou goest the way to thy greatness: it must now be thy best courage that there is no longer any path behind thee!

Thou goest the way to thy greatness: here shall no one steal after thee! Thy foot itself hath effaced the path behind thee, and over it standeth written: Impossibility.

And if all ladders henceforth fail thee, then must thou learn to mount upon thine own head: how couldst thou mount upward otherwise?

Upon thine own head, and beyond thine own heart! Now must the gentlest in thee become the hardest.

He who hath always much-indulged himself, sickeneth at last by his much-indulgence. Praises on what maketh hardy! I do not praise the land where butter and honey – flow!

To learn *to look away from* oneself, is necessary in order to see *many things*: – this hardiness is needed by every mountain-climber.

He, however, who is obtrusive with his eyes as a discerner, how can he ever see more of anything than its foreground!

But thou, O Zarathustra, wouldst view the ground of everything, and its background: thus must thou mount even above thyself – up, upwards, until thou hast even thy stars *under* thee!

Yea! To look down upon myself, and even upon my stars: that only would I call my *summit*, that hath remained for me as my *last* summit! [(Z)]

Creative Will

Where is innocence? Where there is will to procreation. And he who seeketh to create beyond himself, hath for me the purest will. (Z)

Willing emancipateth: for willing is creating: so do I teach. And *only* for creating shall ye learn! (Z)

Willing emancipateth: that is the true doctrine of will and Emancipation – so teacheth you Zarathustra.

No longer willing, and no longer valuing, and no longer creating! Ah, that that great debility may ever be far from me!

And also in discerning do I feel only my will's procreating and evolving delight; and if there be innocence in my knowledge, it is because there is will to procreation in it.

Away from God and gods did this will allure me; what would there be to create if there were – gods!

But to man doth it ever impel me anew, my fervent creative will; thus impelleth it the hammer to the stone. (Z)

Not in *knowledge*, in *creation* lies our salvation! (N)

Creating – that is the great salvation from suffering, and life's alleviation. (Z)

All "It was" is a fragment, a riddle, a fearful chance – until the creating Will saith thereto: "But thus would I have it." – Until the creating Will saith thereto: "But thus do I will it! Thus shall I will it!" (Z)

The *only* happiness lies in creating: all of you should actively *co-create* in every deed in order to grasp *this* happiness! (N)

My suffering and my fellow-suffering – what matter about them! Do I then strive after *happiness*? I strive after my *work*![Z]

Happiness is *not* the goal: but rather the feeling of power. An immense power in man and mankind yearns to *release* itself, yearns to create; it is a continual chain of explosions that have no happiness in sight.[N]

To conquer is the natural consequence of *excessive* power: it is the same as *creation*, as *procreation*, thus the *incorporation* of its own *image* in foreign matter. The higher man must create, and therefore impress his *higher being* upon others...[N]

The drive toward procreation, purpose, the future, the heights is the freedom in all desire. Only in creation is there freedom.[N]

Creating a higher state of being for ourselves is *our* state of being. *To create beyond ourselves*! This is the drive of procreation. This is the drive of action and accomplishment.[N]

Live Dangerously!

Pioneers. – I greet all the signs indicating that a more manly and warlike age is commencing, which will, above all, bring heroism again into honor! For it has to prepare the way for a yet higher age, and gather the force which the latter will one day require, – the age which will carry heroism into knowledge, and *wage war* for the sake of ideas and their consequences. For that end many brave pioneers are now needed, who, however, cannot originate out of nothing, – and just as little out of the sand and slime of present-day civilization and the culture of great cities: men silent, solitary and resolute, who know how to be content and persistent in invisible activity: men who with innate disposition seek in all things that which is *to be overcome* in them: men to whom cheerfulness, patience, simplicity, and contempt of the great vanities belong just as much as do magnanimity in victory and indulgence to the trivial vanities of all the vanquished: men with an acute and independent judgment regarding all victors, and concerning the part which chance has played in the winning of victory and fame: men with their own holidays, their own work-days, and their own periods of mourning; accustomed to command with perfect assurance, and equally ready, if need be, to obey, proud in the one case as in the other, equally serving their own interests: men more imperiled, more productive, more happy! For believe me! – the secret of realizing the largest productivity and the greatest enjoyment of existence is to *live in danger!* (GS)

Heroism. This is the ethos of a people which strives toward a goal against the form it no longer fits. Heroism is the *good will* toward self-destruction. (N)

What makes heroic? – To face simultaneously one's greatest suffering and one's highest hope. (GS)

But by my love and hope I conjure thee: cast not away the hero in thy soul! Maintain holy thy highest hope! (Z)

One has renounced *grand* life, when one has renounced war. [(T)]

Brethren, war's the origin
Of happiness on earth![(GS)]

Translator's Note

My paradise lies "in the shadow of my sword."
– Friedrich Nietzsche, *Ecce Homo.*

Commissioned by the Third Reich, *Schwert des Geists*, or *Sword of the Spirit*, is a mysterious collection of aphorisms by Friedrich Nietzsche which was gathered by a certain Joachim Schondorff and printed by Alfred Kröner Verlag in 1940. The sole purpose of this collection served as an offering to Wehrmacht soldiers on the front lines as the second world war advanced and raged on. It has been out of print since 1941 and was never reprinted in its entirety. Original copies of *Schwert des Geistes*, those that most likely never left the Fatherland, can still be found scattered across Germany in antique bookstores. Those that went to the front were likely riddled with bullets, obliterated by bombs or burned by the soldiers themselves for warmth in the freezing conditions of the Russian front.

Wehrmacht soldiers, ordinary men plucked from their lives of routine and cast into the raging fray, may have known little of Nietzsche and his philosophy, thus did *Schwert des Geistes* provide a firm stepping stone for them to grasp Nietzsche's philosophy, along with a beacon of light as they confronted the bloody wrath and desolation of the war. Throughout his often perilous life, Nietzsche waged philosophical warfare against the "slave morality" rooted in man's longstanding desire to quell the many forms of life's inescapable pain and suffering by means of religion, alcohol and submission to the herd, which he personified via his last man. He thereby created the Superman, born from "master morality," able to take life's struggles, pain and suffering and cultivate something valuable, beautiful and timeless from it. This is the guiding star he created, around which the many constellations of his philosophy shimmer. Nietzsche's emphasis on this is hammered throughout *Schwert des Geistes.*

Fleeting existence and the impermanence of life was their daily reality, yet they were reminded of the lasting mark their deeds can leave on history, along with the problems of a culture that they, as National Socialists, had left behind as they built a new culture for which they were now fighting. They were reminded to aspire to the greatness of the Superman, and not fall victim to the slave morality of the last man. It was never Nietzsche's purpose to bring comfort or console, but to break down constraints within, rebuild and develop the Self. The purpose was to turn the drafted soldier, broken by the horrors of war, into a warrior who would fight with reverence to the full spectrum of life and embrace their life in battle with a whole heart.

Little is known about Schondorff besides the speculation that he was a classics or theater professor in Germany at the time. Books are available under that name on the topics of Greek tragedy and European theatre, but whether it is the same person or not remains speculation. In dissecting and editing the text, a couple of facts came to light: this collection was gathered and printed in haste. Many aphorisms in the original text are attached to mislabeled sources. Additionally, two aphorisms could not be identified in Nietzsche's body of work, not even by the staff at the Nietzsche Dokumentationzentrum in Naumburg. Also, a number of aphorisms were printed with omissions, which are marked with "…". Without knowing why the omissions were done in the first place, the decision was made to leave them as is.

The English translations done by Thomas Common, Anthony Ludovici and Adrian Collins are excellent translations which could not be done any better. Not only did these men possess minds able to understand Nietzsche without the looking glass of political veneer or public opinion, they faithfully conveyed Nietzsche's wit, humor, irony, metaphors, word craft and style beautifully across the language barrier. Their translations are the cream of the crop when it comes to presenting Nietzsche before the Anglo-Saxon world, and are unmatched by any others in form and content.

The sword as a symbol has been assigned a variety of meanings throughout the centuries, to which Nietzsche was no stranger. In his own words he did "delight in drawing the sword" in conjunction with "philosophizing with a hammer," though any reference to the specific phrase *Sword of the Spirit* is not found in Nietzsche's work, thus is a creation of the National Socialists. The cherished warrior poet, playwright and author of the Third Reich, Kurt Eggers, drew heavy influence from Nietzsche in all facets of his work. In his book, *Live Bravely and Die Courageously*, there is mention of a *Sword of the Spirit*. "In the eyes of the tamed down herd people, consciously German people have something demonic, something obsessive about them. One avoids them out of fear for one's own soul, one keeps out of their path, because one hears the sword of their spirit." Perhaps *Schwert des Geistes* was an idea conceived by Eggers and carried out by Schondorff, or Schondorff may have taken the idea and created something entirely different with it.

On the other hand, National Socialist Germany was officially a Christian state with strong ties to the Vatican and Pope Pius XII, as were its fellow axis powers from the Croatian Ustaše to the Belgian Rexist Party. Wehrmacht soldiers wore belt buckles engraved with the phrase *Gott Mit Uns,* God at our side, and it is likely the phrase *Schwert des Geistes* was a reference to the symbolic passage found in the New Testament: "Take the helmet of salvation, and the sword of the spirit, which is the word of God." – Ephesians 6:17. Schondorff likely realized that the ordinary men who made up the Wehrmacht, most of whom, if not all, were Christians, needed a welcoming window into Nietzsche's philosophy, and being that the selection is full of praise for master morality, even "true heathenism," as Nietzsche called it, along with critiques of Christianity, perhaps the purpose of the title was to open the minds of the soldiers, thus allowing them to absorb Nietzsche's words and apply them to their own lives. Nietzsche himself, his strong critiques of Christianity's negative aspects notwithstanding, may have even appreciated the irony of this.

Here are some examples from his work which demonstrate his use of the sword as a symbol and metaphor with varied meanings, both positive and negative, beyond good and evil:

> Such a belief is not angry, it does not find fault, it does not offer resistance; it does not bring "the sword," it has no idea in what respect it might some day separate people. It does not prove itself either by miracles or by reward and promise, or even "by the Scripture:" it is every moment its own miracle, its own reward, its own proof, its own "kingdom of God." *(A)*

> A man who says: "I like that, I take it for my own, and mean to guard and protect it from every one"; a man who can conduct a case, carry out a resolution, remain true to an opinion, keep hold of a woman, punish and overthrow insolence; a man who has his indignation and his sword, and to whom the weak, the suffering, the oppressed, and even the animals willingly submit and naturally belong; in short, a man who is master by nature – when such a man has sympathy, well! that sympathy has value! *(GE)*

> Destroyers, are they who lay snares for many, and call it the state: they hang a sword and a hundred cravings over them. *(Z)*

> "Here are priests: but although they are mine enemies, pass them quietly and with sleeping swords! Even among them there are heroes; many of them have suffered too much – : so they want to make others suffer. Bad enemies are they: nothing is more revengeful than their meekness. And readily doth he soil himself who toucheth them. But my blood is related to theirs; and I want withal to see my blood honored in theirs." *(Z)*

> The four essays composing the Untimely Meditations are thoroughly warlike in tone. They prove that I was no mere

> dreamer, that I delight in drawing the sword – also perhaps, also, that my wrist is dangerously supple. (EH)

> The task is not to overcome opponents in general but only those opponents against whom one has to summon all one's strength, one's skill and one's swordsmanship—in fact to master opponents who are one's equals. (EH)

> "Paradise is under the shadow of a swordsman" – this is also a symbol and a test-word by which souls with noble and warrior-like origin betray and discover themselves. (WP)

Now, as it was then, for readers who know little of Nietzsche, *Sword of the Spirit* serves still as a firm stepping stone to further penetrate and grasp Nietzsche's philosophy, while reminding them that Nietzsche did in fact make it perfectly clear how he felt about a wide range of topics, including the Germany of his day, the Jews, liberalism, slave morality and so forth, with thoughts pregnant with active content, not mere reactive schisms of the herd. For those familiar with Nietzsche in any respect, may this serve as a means to grasping a new understanding of Nietzsche and slough off any yoke of political correctness and public opinion for good and all. Should one desire to further tread the treacherous overgrown path, one need only consult the sources listed, and avoid those rife with the "moralic acid" of the aforementioned yoke, who do nothing but engage in tug of war over a corpse. In his *Will to Power,* Nietzsche realizes the "two possible futures of mankind:

1. Consistent growth of mediocrity.

2. Conscious distinction and self-shaping."

With this *Sword of the Spirit* it is up to you, reader, to decide the future you will have, and how you will live among the last men as civilization, on its current path of disintegration, relives the fall of Rome. Choose wisely, and follow through. The scourge of the modern world will not rest, nevertheless the possibility remains for you to cast off the shackles, own your mind, think your own thoughts, decide your own actions and forge your own life with your own will. Pick up the sword, or cast it aside. Either way, decide.

D. H. W.

Autumn, 2018

www.ingramcontent.com/pod-product-compliance
Lightning Source LLC
Chambersburg PA
CBHW061749270326
41928CB00011B/2432
* 9 7 8 1 9 1 3 1 7 6 6 1 7 *